THE MINISTRY OF

Kings
& Queens
from Laity
to Royalty

Douglas Weiss, Ph.D.

The Ministry of Kings & Queens by Douglas Weiss, Ph.D.
Published by Crown Publishing
P.O. Box 51055
Colorado Springs, CO 80949

Edited by Sharon Hancock and Suzanne Manness
Interior design by Jamie Dodd
Cover design by Michael Saltar, Idea Factory Creative Services

Library of Congress Catalog Card Number: 2004100016
International Standard Book Number: 1-881292-11-8

Dedicated to the Kings and Queens
who were,
who are,
and who are yet to come.

Contents

Introduction

ou are in a church again. That is great! As you sit there, does that feeling of being less than in the Kingdom of God strike again? Do you feel as if there is a professional team, the pastors, missionaries and worship leaders then there is you sitting in the pew? What if you were not merely laity? What if you were actually royalty? Not only royalty but also a king or queen?

When you think of a king, where do your thoughts turn to? Do you think of crowns and jewels or parades and paparazzi? Are kings, in your mind, outdated and have no relevance in North America's modern civilization? If so, you may be in for a surprise. "Kings" and "Queens" are everywhere and are a vital part of the body of Christ. In the pages to come, you will realize that you are kings and queens. Let me explain.

For the purpose of our dialogue, kings and queens or royalty are men and women whose primary sphere of influence is outside the walls of the church or para-church ministry. Priests or the priestly are full-time pastors, missionaries, or para-church employees.

Kings and queens comprise the majority of the local church's membership. They are the employers, business people, and positive social influencers at every level: home, community, national or worldwide. It is for these kings and queens that this book is written.

The Ministry of Kings' and Queens' purpose is to give a language to a movement that is empowering everyday people to fulfill their God-given calling on earth for the kingdom of God. We are not trying to create a new theology, but rather to offer a paradigm to understand the interactivity and interdependence of the priestly church, para-church, and kingly/queenly ministries.

My heart's desire is to express God's high value for such kingly and queenly ministries. Kings and queens' ministries have a myriad of expression, depending on their specific callings and skills. We believe kings and queens have a calling of God in their lives that needs to be identified and fulfilled. My heart is to maximize the interdependent relationship between the kingly ministry and the priestly ministry. I desire a mutual respect shared among those in the kingly , queenly, and priestly aspects of the ministry as we follow God's calling on our lives.

The priestly ministry consists of those in full-time Christian ministry who are mostly pastors, Bible professors, missionaries, and para-church ministries. The priestly receive the tithes and offerings of the kings and queens. The kingly give the tithes and offerings, but their source or sources of income are outside of the church walls in the marketplace of life.

I believe that in the uniting of the priestly and kingly ministries both will be empowered to the highest level possible. I also believe that cities and nations can be won for Christ quicker when these two paradigms of ministry flow together in harmony.

As the kingly or priestly ministries of Christ, we are not to fear, misunderstand, or wrongly judge each other. Rather through the paradigm laid out in this book, we can honor and love one another until death do us part. I believe the marriage of these two ministries lives within the heart of God, and such harmony will produce life-giving results inside and outside the walls of the church.

I earnestly pray that this message brings life to the

kings and queens so that they can identify themselves and follow their personal mandate from God. We have made every effort to honor the priestly on every page. I have humbly submitted this manuscript to the priestly in my life. I want nothing but my love and honor of them to be seen. One of the chapters entitled, "When Kings Come to My Church" is written by one of the leading pastors in our nation, Ted Haggard. Ted Haggard is not only the pastor of a 9,000-member church in Colorado Springs and the president of the National Association of Evangelicals, he is my pastor and friend. I believe he and others serve as positive role models, uniting the kings and priests in a local church that has local, national, and worldwide impact for Christ.

I pray that God may bless all who read *The Ministry of Kings and Queens*. May our Savior, the Lord Jesus Christ, encourage everyone to reach his or her greatest potential for the kingdom and for the glory of God.

Douglas Weiss, Ph.D.

I

In a Day

there comes a day in one's life where change occurs. The Lord our God takes the life of an ordinary man or woman and speaks to them or gives them a revelation or experience that changes their life forever. They become different, altered inside, and from that point on begin a very different journey for their life. I believe that today is such a day.

The Lord is breathing a new word, paradigm, or picture for men and women worldwide. This is the picture of kings/queens and priests. It is being heard and received by kings and queens (royalty) as well as priests around the world. Many who encounter this paradigm are being altered. I know I am one of these whom the Lord God has changed dramatically. He has personally shown me that I am a king, not a priest, and that I should rejoice in my kingly-ness rather than desiring the priesthood in the traditional sense. I, and many other believers—actually most believers—are spiritual royalty after the kingly order of Melchizedek.

Anyway, I am getting ahead of myself. I want to take you on a personal journey of how Jesus has called me into being a king. I am sharing this so that you too can grasp the progressive understanding that culminated in one day for me. Since that day, I have never been the same.

My journey started early in life, never having met my biological father, being placed in various foster homes, experiencing abuse, alcoholism, and addictions. Jesus became an intricate part of my life when I was nineteen. I underwent a dramatic conversion and thirty days later, I was enrolled in a Bible college.

It was here that God began to speak to me. I remember feeling a calling, but I really could not interpret exactly what it was. The "priests" (pastors) in my life believed that Bible school would be a good start. God graciously provided the finances to go to college. It was there that God confirmed prophetic gifting and intercessory prayer within me. I remember reading Acts 2:30, where

12

In a Day

David was called a prophet. I heard God's voice calling me to be a prophet and a king. I had no idea what He was talking about, so I just continued growing in the Lord.

At seminary, I felt that I was significantly different from my peers. I was working toward my Masters in Divinity at the time, intending to go into a full time pastoral ministry. Instead, while still in school, I was given a job at a psychiatric hospital, which challenged me to stay on at the seminary and earn an additional Master's degree in Marriage and Family Counseling. It was during this time that I married my wife Lisa. While working toward my second Master's degree, I left my job at the hospital to become an associate pastor at a local church. Finally, my dream of being in pastoral ministry seemed to be materializing, but for some reason it did not fully satisfy me. All the while God was tugging at my heart in another direction. After much deliberation, I moved into a private counseling practice with the blessings of my church elders since this is where my ministry in the church seemed to flourish.

My counseling practice grew so quickly to the point where I had to hire employees. By the time I graduated from seminary, I had a large private practice, a home, and a satisfying life. I knew I was different but I really did not understand why. I started writing books and publishing. My first real national television appearance was on the "Phil

Donahue Show," and I've since been on "Oprah," "Good
Morning America," "The 700 Club," "Life Today with
James Robison," "TBN," and numerous others.

Our publishing company was growing rapidly and
the counseling center continued to blossom. However,
what about my aching call into the ministry? I would just
rationalize to myself that the books I wrote and my counseling was "ministry," even though these stemmed from a
company rather than a church.

**God spoke to me that these were kings
who had been given unquestionable
authority by God in their realm of influence**

Then Steve Strang entered into my life. Steve owns
Strang Communications, Charisma House Publishing,
"Charisma" magazine, "New Man" magazine, and other
publications. I was speaking at a conference when Steve
asked me to write a book for his publishing company. I
wrote *Intimacy: A 100-Day Guide to Lasting Relationships*, which is a Christian book on attaining intimacy within
a marriage. Steve called me in the midst of this project and
told me that he had been thinking about getting a group of
Christian businessperson together quarterly for idea sharp-
ening. He named the group "Wise Counsel" and invited me

14

to join, along with about ten other businessperson. I really felt the Lord leading me to attend.

When the day came to meet with Steve and the other men, I noticed that the others were ten to twenty years my senior and significantly more financially successful. I felt slightly out of place as they talked openly about their numerous business developments, employees, and the financial aspects that the Lord entrusted to them.

These were not ordinary men. Each had reached the highest level of success in business, yet that was not the impressive part. What was impressive to me was their humility, their love for Jesus, and their obvious spiritual maturity. Each of them had a huge ministry focus in their lives. Each had a national or international outreach for Christ that was incredible.

One man, with just the help of a small support staff that he himself financed, was able to generate and donate over eight million dollars worth of food and other necessities to the poor. One had an international outreach to youth. Another had mission funds and yet another gave away hundreds of thousands of books that he wrote. The list was seemingly endless.

I was enthralled by who these men were in the kingdom of God. As I sat there listening to them, God spoke to me that these were kings who had been given unquestionable authority by God in the realm of their influence. They operated in the gifts of the Spirit and in the fullness of the Word of God. They were financially wealthy but not motivated by money. They were motivated to reach the lost, mature the saints, and meet the social needs God put on their hearts. It was as if each had a unique ministry assignment from God and they were more passionate about their ministries than their businesses.

As one of these fellow Wise Counsel friends said, "I have a deal with God. If I look after His business (ministry) then He will look after mine." This is powerful coming from a man who has several manufacturing plants around the nation.

Since that day I have not had the longing to be a pastor or full-time church staffer. I am a king, not a priest.

This day changed my life. I experienced a total paradigm shift. Observing men, who individually do more than some churches or even denominations could do for Christ, changed something within me. They saw it as imperative to complete their ministry assignments, and not one asked anyone else for the money to do so. They saw the need, figured it out, and paid for it themselves.

In a Day

These are the "kings" God spoke to me about long ago. He then began to speak to me about myself in the role of a king. It started to make sense to me. I operate a couple of relatively successful companies, but my ministry is to heal the brokenhearted. I now travel regularly speaking at conferences on "Intimacy," "Sex, Men and God" and now on the *Ministry of Kings and Queens*, as well. My heart is motivated toward healing others, which is why I write, counsel, and offer media and conferences.

I remember distinctly realizing on the plane ride home from my first Wise Counsel meeting that the pull to be in the ministry was gone. Since that day, I have not had the longing to be a pastor or full-time church staffer. I am a king, not a priest.

It was as is if my eyes were opened. I could see myself the way God sees me, as a king. I was given a true calling. I am able to utilize my giftings for what He has designed me for. I am as holy, righteous, and pleasing to God as anyone in full-time ministry is.

Neither priest nor king is more special than the other one. God does not rank one's work as being more special or holy than the other. As a king, I can be just as obedient and pleasing to my Lord as any priestly (pastoral) person can be.

It is hard to put in print how I felt, but I was free

from trying to be something I was not supposed to be. I am not a pastor, but rather a king without shame. I can teach the Word of God, be used for miracles, disciple people, and do a great job at the office, and all are pleasing to God. I have been permanently changed. I no longer feel inferior or superior to my priestly friends. I still meet with the Wise Counsel group. They understand me. We talk the same language, solve problems the same way, and are challenged by each other to go for what God has assigned us to accomplish. Dreams are acceptable, goals are reachable, and with kings as friends, all of us can do more for the kingdom of God.

That is how I started on this journey of accepting myself as a king. I had to get rid of some old religious paradigms and release some of the Word of God. I read the Bible differently now as a king without priestly glasses.

In walking through this awakening, I learned to keep notes. As the message of the ministry of kings evolved, I would share it with other kings and priests throughout the country. The lights would go on and we would have long conversations.

Since it was evident to my group that God was giving me insight on these things, I was encouraged to write a book about it. I in no way have the corner on under-standing this new paradigm of kings and priests, but I believe that both kings and priests need each other in this hour of the church.

I believe that if kings and priests can understand one another better—and more importantly honor one another—then together the kingdom will advance greater than at any other time in history.

II

The New Order of Royalty

 will never forget the night the Lord gave me the revelation of Melchizedek. I was traveling to Naples, Florida, to speak at a conference on intimacy in marriage. On the flight, I took a nap, had time to pray, and finally arrived close to midnight. I was still wide-awake because of my rest, so I asked the Lord what He would have me read. He told me Genesis 14. I thought, *Okay great, a good bedtime story from God.* What happened next changed my life forever.

What God was going to show me in His Word, while alone in that hotel room, was something I have never seen or heard in more than twenty years with Him, including four years of Bible college and over five years of seminary. The subject? The ministry of kings and queens is a topic on which I have specifically sought God's insight.

Go with me to Genesis 14 for just a little background information. There was a great war where five kings fought against four kings, back in the days of Abram (before God renamed him). Custom dictated that when an army overcame an enemy, they would take the spoils and plunder from those who lost the battle. Among the silver, gold, clothes and horses were also people, commonly captured by the victors. In this particular account, herded in with the captured was one who was dear to Abram's heart, his nephew Lot. Lot lived in Sodom and was part of the bounty of Kedorlaomer, the king who had won the battle.

When Abram heard that Lot was a captive, he did what any king or queen would do who saw a social injustice: He had a committee meeting! Actually, Abram was a king and kings do not usually utilize committees. He rounded up his employees of "trained men," which totaled three hundred. These men overcame Kedorlaomer, and Abram rescued his nephew. These were great men who assisted Abram and helped him change the injustice done to Lot.

Here is where the story gets interesting. Abram and

his employees were on their way back in the valley of Shaveh, known as "the valley of kings." The king of Sodom, who was defeated by Kedorlaomer meets Abram, and soon Melchizedek, the king of Salem, shows up as well.

Melchizedek brought out bread and wine. During the meal, this king of Salem, who was also a priest of the God Most High, blessed Abram.

The Melchizedek order is part of God's unchanging nature, and He desires for us to understand how to function as kings and queens.

Abram responded by giving a tithe to Melchizedek. Abram also gave the rest of the spoils back to the king of Sodom, minus his employees' share for their efforts. As a side note here about Abram's giving, he gave to two other kings, the king/priest Melchizedek and another king. Secondly, Abram acts here as only an emotionally and financially secure king would in this situation.

He fought a battle and won, but he gave the bounty away so that a secular king could not boast about how he made Abram wealthy. Abram wanted God to get the glory for his wealth. As I observe today's kings, I notice the similarities in that they fight social injustice here and abroad without compensation. I love the way these kings and queens think.

I want to share with you more of this new order and why Melchizedek, king of Salem, is a prototype of God's will for believers. This king/priest model is clearly laid out in Hebrews 6-8. In verses 6:17-20 we have the writer of Hebrews expressing why this kingly priest is so important for the heirs of salvation to understand.

[17]Because God wanted to make the unchanging nature of his purpose very clear to the heirs of what was promised, he confirmed it with an oath. [18]God did this so that, by two unchangeable things in which it is impossible for God to lie, we who have fled to take hold of the hope offered to us may be greatly encouraged. [19]We have this hope as an anchor for the soul, firm and secure. It enters the inner sanctuary behind the curtain, [20]where Jesus, who went before us, has entered on our behalf. He has become a high priest forever, in the order of Melchizedek. (Hebrews 6:17-20)

In verse 17, we can clearly see that in revealing the Melchizedek kingly/priestly order, God wanted to illustrate "the unchanging nature of His purpose." He wanted us as believers to know there is a nature in a kingly/priestly order that is unchanging. I think as you walk through the Bible you can see this happening with Moses (kingly) and Aaron (priestly), and with kings and high priests in Old Testament government. This is also illustrated in the life of Christ, a carpenter, self-employed businessman and minister of the gospel, as well as a sacrifice for sins.

This Melchizedek order is part of God's unchanging nature, and He desires for us to understand how to function as kings and queens. The writer continues to offer support as to why this is so important. In verse 18, if we understand God's oath, His purpose is that we would be greatly encouraged. I can tell you personally since I have come to understand the kingly priesthood that I have been radically encouraged. So encouraged that I realize I don't have to be a pastor, missionary or seminary professor to please God and be in His perfect will.

Verse 19 talks about having this hope as an anchor for our soul. Hope is a great thing for kings and queens. When you know you are loved for who you are and that your talents are acceptable and desirable to God, security can reign in such a way that hope springs forth.

In Hebrews 6:20, Jesus has become a high priest forever in the order of Melchizedek. It is so important that kings understand that the order of Melchizedek is a kingly order, not a Levitical or priestly order. This order of priest's is kingly not just priestly.

As we walk through the upcoming Scriptures, I pray the spirit of revelation flows through your heart and minds. I believe if you receive the revelation of the Melchizedek order, every business owner, employee, stay-at-home mom, or anyone who is not a full-time minister, will be released, encouraged, and have so much more hope in life because you will realize your high value to the Almighty God who loves you just the way you are. Let us read Hebrews 7:1-4:

This Melchizedek was king of Salem and priest of God Most High. He met Abraham returning from the defeat of the kings and blessed him, ¹and Abraham gave him a tenth of everything. First, his name means "king of righteousness"; then also, "king of Salem" means king of peace." ²Without father or mother, without begin-ning of days or end of life, like the Son of God he remains a priest forever. ³Just think how great he was: Even the patriarch Abraham gave him a tenth of the plunder. (Hebrews 7:1-4)

The writer of Hebrews in verse 6:20 states that Jesus has become a priest like Melchizedek. Then in verses

7:1-4 he begins to define Melchizedek as a king (also see Genesis 14:18). Verse 7:2 gives three definitions of Melchizedek's name that all include an aspect of his kingship: king of righteousness, king of Salem and king of peace.

This is the new order of the priesthood that God has in mind, a Melchizedek, kingly priesthood rather than a Levitical priesthood. God allowed His only Son to be a self-employed businessperson (carpenter), a king with a ministry to the world. It is very important to keep this in mind as we walk through a new priestly order that is kingly. It is the employee, employer, and business owner who God also has in mind to minister the kingdom of righteousness.

The next aspect the writer turns to in chapter 7 is how great this Melchizedek was. In verse 4 we read, "Just think how great he was: Even the patriarch Abraham gave him a tenth of the plunder." In verse 7 the writer states, *"And without doubt the better person is blessed by the greater."* We clearly know Abraham was a king, as he was so blessed that he and Lot had to move away from each other. Abraham's band of employees overcame the kings in Genesis 14. Therefore Abraham, a great king, gave to a man who he perceived to be a greater king. Let us read Genesis 14:5-10.

[5]In the fourteenth year, Kedorlaomer and the kings allied with him went out and defeated the Rephaites in Ashteroth Karnaim, the Zuzites in Ham, the Emites in Shaveh Kiriathaim [6]and the Horites in the hill country of Seir, as far as El Paran near the deser [7]Then they turned back and went to En Mishpat (that is, Kadesh), and they conquered the whole territory of the Amalekites, as well as the Amorites who were living in Hazazon Tamar.

[8]Then the king of Sodom, the king of Gomorrah, the king of Admah, the king of Zeboiim and the king of Bela (that is, Zoar)marched out and drew up their battle lines; the Valley of Siddim [9]against Kedorlaomer king of Elam, Tidal king of Goiim, Amraphel king of Shinar and Arioch king of Ellasar—four kings against five. [10]Now the Valley of Siddim was full of tar pits, and when the kings of Sodom and Gomorrah fled, some the men fell into them and the rest fled to the hills. (Genesis 14:5-10)

I know you have probably heard sermons about how Abraham paid tithes. I encourage you to read this and think through what the writer is really trying to say.

The New Order of Royalty

1) Abraham (king) paid tithes to a greater king, Melchizedek.

2) Levi was in Abraham, so in fact Levi (the priestly) paid tithes to the kingly order of priest, Melchizedek.

This amazes me that the kingly order of priest, the Melchizedek order, received tithes from the Levitical. I think it may be awhile before we see those in the pastoral (priestly) role give money to those in kingly positions to accomplish ministry. What a day that will be when the full-time preacher empowers the kingly financially to do the ministry that the kingly or queenly has received from God.

Hear my heart: I am not recommending that the kingly not tithe to the local church, which is the body of Christ on earth. I believe tithing is just the beginning, and most kings I know give much more than a tithe. I just think it is utterly amazing that the writer of Hebrews went to the greatest lengths to illustrate this kingly order of priesthood. This new order is the prototype of what God desires for most of us as believers.

The writer continues to push this point home as he points out that Christ did not come through a Levitical bloodline, and the fact that Jesus' priesthood was completely different.

As you read the rest of Hebrews 7 and part of chapter 8, you will notice an outline start to emerge, portraying Jesus as a different priest, a better sacrifice, and the fulfillment of a better covenant. I want to emphasize what is not usually emphasized. This kingly, priestly order is what God is looking for today!

God is looking for businesspeople of every level to identify with this kingly/queenly priesthood. You are part of God's will on the earth. As you work and labor among the lost, you can witness, do miracles, and provide for the weak and hurting in your area and around the world.

Let us go a little further with this concept. When Jesus decided to gather His disciples, He chose twelve businesspeople. He did not choose one priest. He simply wanted men who were teachable and able to get things done. Several of these men were well enough off financially and able to take care of their families at home while going on the road with Jesus. They were kings, not priests.

Jesus himself lived, and selected men who lived the kingly, priestly model of ministry. Jesus worked hard at Joseph's carpentry business. As the oldest son, after Joseph died—somewhere between Jesus' twelfth and thirtieth birthdays—the responsibility of running the family business fell to Him. He and his brothers ran a company that we can reasonably assume was successful. It may have also given Jesus the financial freedom to be able to do His ministry for over a three-year period.

Your calling to the Melchizedek order may mean that you function as a businessperson, employee, or any other role in society, but your heart burns for touching other lives. You do not have to go to Bible college or seminary to fulfill your destiny or calling in Christ.

Accepting our roles as kings and queens puts purpose to the daily adventure and responsibilities of life.

The Melchizedek order, is creative, resourceful and practical, and is a new real order of God. If the priestly of our day (pastors, etc.) can come alongside, support and encourage the Melchizedek order (congregation), we will see the greatest outpouring of Christ in the nations to date.

I believe it is this order of kingly and queenly priests God had in mind throughout history. The common man or woman saved by Christ is anointed and empowered to do the miracles of Christ in their sphere of influence.

When you understand your kingdom in Christ, many things can happen. You will begin to take your job, business or home much more seriously. After all, you are a king or queen, and you are 100 percent responsible; the buck stops with you and your talents.

Does not the parable of the talent make more sense to you now? Remember in Matthew 25:15 Jesus tells the story of three servants who were given money. One received five talents, the second three, and the last received one. The servants with five talents and three talents doubled their master's money. This was probably done through risk and lots of hard work. As a result, they received double portions because they took their talents responsibly. They received authority over cities because of their business savvy.

However, the lazy, fearful servant was not blessed because he did not realize he was 100 percent responsible, and he gave himself excuses as to why he could not produce for the master. This is how so many people behave if they see themselves as laity and not royalty.

I say this to encourage you. We kings and queens can receive opportunities and authority never imagined if we are kingly responsible. Accepting our roles as kings and queens puts purpose to the daily adventure and responsibilities of life. We are in training, and if we are responsible, we can produce so much good for ourselves and for others.

As kings and queens, you are God's first line of defense and protection on the earth. You are not second fiddle, although you may have believed that you were. You are the first order on the earth to make a miraculous difference.

If you receive your calling as the Melchizedek king/queen that you are, then the power of spiritual life can flow through you. So many kings and queens have only to be awakened to the fact that they are primary in the kingdom and just need to mature in their ministry.

The ministry of Christ, the Melchizedek order priest, is yours. Do not long for the pastoral team of God if it is not your calling. Let them abound in their own priestly ministry. You have a different calling. Get the kingdom of God on the earth through the gifts God gave you. Support the priestly, but do not minimize your calling as a king or queen.

The Levitical, pastoral priesthood of our day is to cheer, lead you on, empower you, give spiritual feeding through the Word and their lives, and keep up with all you are doing.

On the other hand, kings and queens are not just to pay a tithe and that is the end of "our ministry." Our ministry for God is to be Christ on the earth so that others can inherit the gospel. You have a ministry in your church, community, state, nation or world. Be encouraged, that you are a king or queen on the earth.

Can you imagine the day when the church is 97

percent muscle because kings and queens in congregations are performing their ministry? Contrast that to the current situation where 97 percent of the kingly congregation watch the three percent perform their weekly Levitical service ministry. Wow! Wouldn't that be closer to what Jesus had in mind?

Can you imagine such a day? I can imagine it in my church, because one out of ten is leading a ministry cell group. The kings and queens can do the ministry. When they are empowered and acting on their calling, cities will come to Christ.

I pray that you will pick up your Melchizedek calling as a kingly priest, and seek God. Proverbs 25:2 states, *"It is the glory of God to conceal a matter; to search out a matter is the glory of kings."* It is the glory of a *king* to seek out a matter. Find why God called you into this kingly priesthood and get to it. There is so much adventure when you become immersed in the kingly and queenly ministry God has given you.

III

Royal Commands

od's Word is great! In His wisdom, He wrote clear directions for kings. From the Scriptures we as modern kings and queens can draw some commandments, not guidelines, for our lives. We find both "thou shalt nots" and "thou shalts" in the book of Deuteronomy.

Let us look at a section at a time. We will start in Deut. 17:14-15:

[14]When you enter the land the Lord your God is giving you and have taken possession of it and settled in it, and you say, "Let us set a king over us like all the

nations around us," ¹⁵be sure to appoint over you the king the Lord your God chooses. He must be from among your own brothers. Do not place a foreigner over you, one who is not a brother Israelite. (Deut. 17:14-15)

This is the first commandment to the Israelites about kings. A king was first to be selected by God. They were not to vote or have any other such process, but rather God Himself was to decide who was to be king. This could not be done at this time in Israel's history because ideally they were a theocracy.

This king was to be a brother, not a foreigner. This is radically important because a brother understands the local and national circumstances. After all, this is his homeland. In America, we still hold to our president being a resident. Many nations adhere to this policy of choosing a resident to be their leader.

Kings are local people who went to the local school, worked small jobs and blossomed. I love this localness of kings. They seem to have an ability to root and grow where they are. Many kings and queens also have a territorial understanding of their ministry and influence in that area. People trust you when they have known you for twenty years. They also know your children, and can laugh about the good old days with you.

The following kingly commands—thou shalt nots—are directly for the king himself. I really believe a king or queen who lives within these basic guidelines can have a great quality of life. I think God made these commands relatively simple to understand. Kings and queens generally do not like being told what to do or not to do, but in this case, it is essential they heed these commands from God. After all, they are written by the King of Kings, not just a man with a good idea.

Kingly Commandment 1: *"The king moreover, must not acquire great numbers of horses for himself or make the people return to Egypt to get more of them for the Lord has told you "You are not to go back that way again." (Deut. 17:16)*

The fact that God is so specific here is important. The king was not to acquire many horses for himself. I think this commandment has at least two major facets for us as modern-day kings and queens. First, the king was not to be confident in his natural strength. Horses in the Old Testament culture were significant in determining the might of one's army. This concept concurs with the Psalms:

[16]*"No king is saved by the size of his army; no warrior escapes by his great strength. [17]A horse is a vain hope for deliverance; despite all it's great strength it cannot save." (Psalm 33:16-17)*

Also, remember the discipline David received from the Almighty God when he wanted to look at his own strength and counted Israel:

[2]*So the king said to Joab and the army commanders with him, "Go throughout the tribes of Israel from Dan to Beersheba and enroll the fighting men, so that I may know how many there are." [3]But Joab replied to the king, "May the Lord your God multiply the troops a hundred times over, and may the eyes of my lord the king see it. But why does my lord the king want to do such a thing?"*

[4]*The king's word, however, overruled Joab and the army commanders; so they left the presence of the king to enroll the fighting men of Israel. [5]After crossing the Jordan, they camped near Aroer, south of the town in the gorge, and then went through Gad and on to Jazer. [6]They went to Gilead and the region of Tahtim Hodshi, and on to Dan Jaan and around toward Sidon. [7]Then*

they went toward the fortress of Tyre and all the towns of the Hivites and Canaanites. Finally, they went on to Beersheba in the Negev of Judah.

[8]After they had gone through the entire land, they came back to Jerusalem at the end of nine months and twenty days. [9]Joab reported the number of the fighting men to the king: In Israel there were eight hundred thousand able-bodied men who could handle a sword, and in Judah five hundred thousand. [10]David was conscience-stricken after he had counted the fighting men, and he said to the Lord, "I have sinned greatly in what I have done. Now, O Lord, I beg you, take away the guilt of your servant. I have done a very foolish thing."

[11]Before David got up the next morning, the word of the Lord had come to Gad the prophet, David's seer: [12]"Go and tell David, 'This is what the Lord says: I am giving you three options. Choose one of them for me to carry out against you." [13]So Gad went to David and said to him, "Shall there come upon you three years of famine in your land? Or three months of fleeing from your enemies while they pursue you? Or three days of plague in your land? Now then, think it over and decide how I should answer the one who sent me."

[14]David said to Gad, "I am in deep distress. Let us fall into the hands of the Lord, for his mercy is great; but do not let me fall into the hands of men." [15]So the Lord sent a plague on Israel from that morning until the end of the time designated, and seventy thousand of the people from Dan to Beersheba died. (2 Samuel 24:2-15)

Look at the consequences of a king who decided to look away from God and His supernatural source of strength, and neglected to depend on God fully. In our positions as kings and queens, God will provide us with resources, but he does not want our hearts to trust in these resources above Him. These resources can be talents, wisdom, charisma, or beauty and are great to have, but a king or queen does not rely on them, but rather they rely on God alone as their only strength.

If a king or queen gives his or her heart to collecting these symbols and begins to look to them for identity and purpose, there is a problem.

This leads to the second facet of not acquiring many horses. Horses were just symbols. Symbols can be a tricky obstacle for our hearts. If a symbol becomes a way of defining worldly success, a king or queen can spend too much time acquiring more of them.

Western culture, is full of success images, icons and symbols. In our material culture these can be the size of your house, how many houses you own and their location, where you go on vacation, where your kids go to school, what kind of car you drive, or whose name is on your clothes.

The symbols themselves may not be inherently evil. However if a king or queen gives their heart to collecting these symbols and begins to look to them for identity and purpose, there is a problem. Kings and queens are often blessed and consequently can have access to and enjoy many of the "symbols" of success. The trick is not to let these symbols occupy the throne of your heart. When the location of your home or the make of your vehicle or other worldly symbols become what your heart depends on for solace, strength or affirmation, you are in trouble.

God Himself wants to be that voice of affirmation to our heart. He wants to mold our identity on our trust and love for Him and His love and trust of us. You are His king or queen regardless of the size of any symbol in your life at this point. The point is, be careful not to seek symbols; rather, "Seek first His kingdom and His righteousness, and all these things will be given to you as well" (Matt. 6:33). If your heart priority is straight then the kingly and queenly life will not hurt you or your relationship with God.

Kingly Commandment 2: *He must not take many wives, or his heart will be led astray. (Deut. 17:17a)*

This second command may look easy, but in the culture in which it was given, it was quite difficult. At this time, women were ranked slightly above animals. Women were given as gifts like horses. In the realm of kings, often a wife would be given to a king for a peace symbol or as a thank you from other kings. This is an important issue for a king's heart. Regardless of how wise your heart is, it can be turned away from God as Solomon's heart was. Solomon had many wives and concubines. He was by far the wisest of men, and yet his wives (many were foreign) turned his heart away from the one true God.

You are probably thinking that this one is easy for us Westerners. Most of us may appear monogamous or maybe have two or three wives or husbands through divorces. Maybe technically this would be true but I think this issue goes deeper. The first command of a king is to protect his heart from lust for more and more, from moving dependency upon God to something else. If you live in a culture as king and believe you can arbitrarily have any person you want, I believe the risk of lusting after women and acquiring them as objects in your mind, heart and in reality can become a part or full-time pursuit. Think of the time Solomon wasted just in marriage ceremonies alone! At least two and a half years if you consider that a ceremony took up most of a day.

As a counselor, I have been privileged for over sixteen years to work with the kingly. I have seen kingly who were worth over $50 million, CEOs, doctors, lawyers, entertainers, entrepreneurs and employees at every level. A common issue the kingly have to guard against is sexual lust. Lust for power, control, and money can be issues for kings. Yet the sexual lust I have seen repeatedly has trapped these kings and limited their destiny and ministry.

Kings and queens by nature do not like boundaries or "Thou shalt nots," but unfortunately; in the area of sexual lust God has very firm rules for everyone, kings and queens included. Lust is deadly. In James 1:15, lust evolves through three stages: Lust, sin and death. Even the kingly cannot avoid this. If a king or queen feeds their heart with lust, they will eventually pursue it.

In the Tenth Commandment, the Lord our God states, "You shalt not covet (another word for lust) your neighbors wife." Almost every woman you meet is or will be another man's wife. We are not permitted as people of

God, male or female, to lust.

This goes even deeper. I believe the enemy of our soul has a particular plan to trap good people, especially kings, in sexual sin. It plays out in the lives of many of the kings I have worked with.

When a king is a boy, between twelve to fifteen years old, the enemy tempts him with sexual fantasy and/or pornography. This young boy takes the bait of sexual lust. This lust is then brought into his self-sex (masturbation) life. What the boy does not know is that every time he has a sexual release with his fantasy, he releases the highest chemical reward his body has to offer. This chemical high of endorphins or enkephalins attaches this boy to whatever he is viewing, pornography or fantasy. Over a short period, he develops a neurological pathway that rewards him for lust and viewing "many wives."

If he continues this disconnected, lustful reinforcement lifestyle with pornography, he can struggle with lust and inappropriate sexual behavior, like adultery, prostitution, or homosexuality, depending on his fantasy object for the rest of his life. In my book, *Sex, Men & God*, I go into detail about all of this information. I think every king and queen should read *Sex, Men & God* to understand this aspect of male sexuality.

If a man marries and continues to view pornography

and masturbate to fantasy, he is having his "many wives." His heart is full of lust and endless images. His sex life with his wife is less satisfying because of his repetition of lust. He can even become sexually addicted.

If you find yourself trapped in this situation and you want to get free, I have personally helped many kings get and stay free from "many wives." I would encourage you to get the books *The Final Freedom: Pioneering Sexual Addiction Recovery* and *101 Freedom Exercises: A Christian Guide to Sexual Addiction Recovery*. You can go to our website at www.intimatematters.com to receive free newsletters for further help.

Be encouraged: Freedom is possible. I have seen so many kings restored to a better walk with God, better relationships with their wife and family, and their God-given destiny returned. An interesting thing to note is that with kings who control their own income—business owners, entrepreneurs and salespeople, for example—they have shown to double their income the first year of healing just about every time.

I have seen many kings who have taken into their heart "many wives," given themselves over to their lust and have come close to losing everything. If you struggle with this issue, get help immediately so you can be free to be the king you were called to be. Do not let shame and fear steal your destiny and authority.

"To him who overcomes and does my will to the end, I will give authority over the nations." (Rev. 2:25)

You, as a king, or queen are a major part of God's plan on the earth. It is on your shoulders revival will or will not happen in your area of influence. The enemy knows this. If you allow your "many wives" issue to take you down, many may not inherit the kingdom of God. You are important enough to heal, so go for it!

Kingly Commandment 3: *"He must not accumulate large amounts of silver and gold." (Deut. 17:17b)*

At first glance, this command can seem odd. How can a king be a king if he does not have large amounts of silver and gold? I do not think that this is what is being addressed. Of course, for the kingdom that he (or she) is king over, he is to create wealth, industry, and jobs. To do such things a king must have some wealth to begin with.

However, the king was not to concentrate on personal wealth. That wealth was to serve a purpose for the greater good of others, not just self.

This flies smack in the face of the current trends of

materialism, even in the Christian world. We can often find ourselves trying harder to get more and climbing the ladder. Now do not get me wrong. I am not advocating that wealth by itself is bad or evil. If that were true, Abraham would have been considered bad as well as hundreds of others in the Bible and church history. After all, wealth builds churches, sends missionaries, and keeps every radio, TV and print ministry spreading the gospel. Wealth is wealth; what we do with it and what it does to our heart is the issue. I believe these commandments for kings and queens are all designed to protect their hearts. Kings and queens are heart people: If their heart moves then they are already equipped with the focus, determination and creativity to get anything done that they put their heart into.

If wealth gets the heart of a king or queen and it becomes the reason they live, instead of living for Christ and being His servant on earth, they can become spiritually void and callous to the true reason for their wealth, which is others. Kings and queens are put on earth or in the church of Jesus Christ to fulfill His purposes.

Our wealth as kings or queens is not to be our focus. We are obediently to use our wealth in service to the church, the local or worldwide community.

I find it interesting as I am around fully developed kings and queens living in total financial abundance that they all seem to have a genuine handle on the issue of wealth. Many have foundations that they personally fund to help the poor in their city or across the world. Some minister to youth or seniors. I remember having breakfast with a king who is a real estate developer. We were talking about wealth and giving. He informed me about a foundation he had for a certain country. He said, "That's my country. I'm responsible for it." He went on to tell me that his wife also has a foundation for a different country and how she felt responsible before God for that country.

Kings and queens can do great things as long as they understand that their wealth is to be used for the sake of others, not just for the bigger, better toys, houses, or extras. You can have them, but they are not the purpose of your wealth.

Kings and queens can do great things as long as they understand that their wealth is to be used for the sake of others, not just for the bigger, better toy.

Wealth without a purpose can end in arrogance and waste, and can ruin a king or queen in the kingdom. The absolute joy that fills your heart when God shows you the purpose of your wealth is overwhelming. The fact that one person who is doing their job, running their business, can change a child's life, a family, a city, a nation, or several nations is incredible!

Ask God where your heart is on the issue of wealth. Why do you have it? Why do you keep getting more and more? What is your responsibility for your wealth? Who is to be touched? When you answer these questions, you will come in to something much greater than yourself and the joy of being a king or queen will flood your soul like never before.

Often the answer to what you are to do with your wealth answers another question: "Why am I on planet earth?" When you know the why, peace can enter your heart.

A king or queen acknowledges that all wealth comes from God and that he or she is a steward of wealth, not an owner. As a steward and servant, wealth flows through kings and queens doing the bidding of the King of Kings, our Lord and Savior Jesus Christ.

Kingly Commandment 4: [18]*When he takes the throne of his kingdom, he is to write for himself on a scroll a copy of this law, taken from that of the priests, who are Levites.* [19]*It is to be with him, and he is to read it all the days of his life so that he may learn to revere the Lord* *his God and follow carefully all the words of this law and these decrees* [20]*and not consider himself better than his brothers and turn from the law to the right or to the left. Then he and his descendants will reign a long time over his kingdom in Israel. (Deut. 17:18-20)*

This commandment is a "do" command as opposed to a "Thou shalt not." Kings and queens are to read the Word of God daily. We are influenced by the thoughts, words, and boundaries of God. A king or queen is to have what is commonly called a quiet time, regardless of their schedule or how important or powerful he or she feels they are. Every royal must submit him or herself to the Word of God daily. This is critical for their spiritual growth and grounding.

Many kings and queens operate with a gift of wisdom. They intuitively see opportunity or understand an issue, but this gift is not to be their anchor. The Word of God is to be their anchor. A king or queen without daily time with God and His word can begin to rule the people he or she influences out of the flesh, not the thoughts, Word of God or Spirit of God.

The humbling of ourselves daily is to serve four primary purposes for the kingly and queenly. First, in Deut. 17:19, "so he may learn to revere the Lord." A king or queen who fears God is useful. A king or queen who has no fear of God will be destroyed. If a king or queen is not in the Word of God, the fear or reverence of God will not abide in them.

The book of Proverbs says the fear of the Lord is the beginning of wisdom. If you do not fear God enough to get daily in his Word, you will not be fulfilled as a king or queen and may never reach your full destiny of influence.

There are few things worse than a businessperson, employee or parent who operates in the flesh on a regular basis and call themselves a Christian. As kings and queens, we are commanded to read the Bible daily. We cannot look to the priestly (pastors, teachers) only to feed us; we are to feed ourselves. I would encourage you to make this a top priority daily. Place reading the Word on your Day-timer, Palm Pilot, calendar or refrigerator.

Priests and pastors are a great benefit to a king and queen's spiritual growth, but if that is where you get most of your spiritual food, you are not acting as a king or queen. Kings and queens hear from God, kings and queens read the Bible, kings and queens do not make excuses; they make a plan. If you rest on your spiritual laurels and look at your success as validation of your spiritual maturity, you are truly deceived and disobedient as a king or queen. Rise up and read the Word daily. Keep track of it if you need to, but get this done so you can walk in reverence of your God. He is worthy of this and you are worthy to be the best possible.

Being a king or queen does not guarantee you will automatically be a good one in your family, church or culture. Bad kings fill the pages of the Bible. They did not seek or revere God, nor did they read His Word daily as they were commanded. Your daily walk in the Word of God influences the kind of king or queen you are.

The second purpose of reading the Bible daily is found in the rest of verse 19: *"...and follow carefully all the word of this law and these decrees."* The second purpose deals with the issues of authority and obedience.

Kings and queens need something greater than themselves. The Word of God is to be obeyed. Regardless of your kingly influence, you must obey the Word of God. The Word of God commands that we love others, love our spouse, be kind to our children and above all, to be honest. The Bible is our final authority.

Kings and queens with the humility to obey God's Word can become fully developed in influencing others. Kings and queens are often given a domain and authority in an area or arena but they are not authorities unto themselves. God Himself will deal with a king or queen who does not obey the Word of God as a Christian. *"God resists the proud but gives grace to the humble" (James 4:6).* We are not God. We must obey what we know of the word in character, in giving, in business and in marriage. Remember the verse, *"To obey is better than sacrifice" (1 Samuel 15:22).* That verse was directed at a king who directly disobeyed the Word of God stating that a priest was to offer a sacrifice not a king. He was disobedient, and from this act forward, Saul began to lose his kingly domain.

The third purpose for kings in reading the Word of God daily is found in Deut. 17:20: *"And not consider himself better than his brother and turn from the law to the right or to the left."* This really can easily become an obstacle for kings and queens. You are being blessed; God is giving to you supernatural opportunities. Your peers are in awe of what God is doing. It is easy to feel you had something to do with this, and that you are "special." Staying in the Word of God allows God to reassure you of His love for you and His equal love for those you serve and influence.

We are all dust and to dust we will return, according to Genesis 3. We should not think too highly of ourselves. We have reproduced life, but we have never "created" new life forms or made one blade of grass grow. We are not so great compared to our Creator. Being a king or queen is God's choice. If He has not called you into full-time ministry in a pastoral, missionary, Bible teacher sense, you are kingly. All your brothers and sisters in Christ are also kingly. They are just as valuable to the kingly purposes of God on the earth as you are.

You have your family, church, business, friends and society to influence for Christ and they have theirs. You may be a big shot in your own world, almost famous, but the queen right next to you in the pew may have a greater influence on her soccer team with children than you will ever have on them.

Reading the Word of God daily allows you to stay grounded and humble. Every child of God is worthy of honor and respect because God has chosen them. Wealth or influence makes you no more loved or worthy of Christ's blood. The Word of God cautions queens and us kings against this pride repeatedly. This sin of superiority is a slippery one for kings or queens. The more developed you become as a king or queen the more on guard you must be of this enemy of pride.

The last purpose for reading the Word of God daily is in the second part of Deut. 17:20. *"Then he and his descendents will reign a long time over his kingdom in Israel."* The fact of having a daily quiet time of getting God's Word in our spiritual belly has generational blessings. I think that alone is worth getting in the Word!

Royal Commands

Think about it. If your child sees you read the Bible, pray to the Almighty God, stay humble and faithful to your spouse without lust for others, not using your money just for you, sees you modeling a wealth for others type of lifestyle and obeying God's Word while confessing your sins, they will see a great role model they can duplicate. Whether they become nurses, lawyers, employees or follow you in your sphere of influence, they will know how to embrace the kingly or even the priestly ministry God has for them.

This type of spiritual inheritance is so much greater than wealth. Most wealth does not go down a family tree as far as Godly character does. You are the link to generations of godly kings and priests. I think it is worth blessing our generations by staying in the Word daily, not collecting too many symbols of success, being sexually pure and faithful and having right attitudes and behaviors toward wealth.

God wants to protect our hearts as kings and queens. It is His desire to have us have these few but direct boundaries. Whether we are local-influence kings or international businessperson, we all need boundaries to be successful kings or queens in our sphere of influence. God's revival depends on kings and queens (not just pastors) being obedient. Those in the kingly or queenly ministry must prepare themselves to obey so we can bring the harvest into the church of Jesus Christ. We are the ones in the marketplace where the lost are. So be encouraged as a king or queen. Great ministry and blessings are ahead of you as you obey the commandments given specifically to kings and queens.

IV

Royal Intercession

he Bible discusses intercession often throughout its many pages. As I pondered this with the glasses of the kingly/priestly concepts, I came to a stark awareness that I feel is compelling. Many people reading a book on kings and queens think of the battles, the wealth, and the power to influence for good and evil, but I believe there is even a greater power given to the kings of the earth that many have never accessed.

This power is the power of intercession. It is the ability to have God's ear and heart when you pray for those in your sphere of influence. The God of heaven and earth listens to the hearts of kings and queens. There are several biblical examples where God literally harkens to the prayer of kings and in some cases even changes world events.

There are men and women like you and me who are everyday business-people. Moses, who was a prince of Egypt (public servant), turned to a professional herdsman, a king chosen by God (remember Aaron was the priest). The twelve tribes of Israel only had one tribe that was priestly; all the others were kingly tribes.

Wow! When you understand that most of the Bible was written about the kingly, it is remarkable. We are one of the major players of God's Spirit, callings and anointings on the earth. The common market place people are within God's plan. The priestly role is available to support and encourage us.

I say all this as a preparation for intercession because the kings and queens are everywhere in the Bible. They are the ones that God is depending on in the last days.

As kings and queens, we have great intercessory authority.

Let us look at some prime examples of God directly responding to various kings in the Bible who ventured to intercede for those in their sphere of influence. Then I want to take you through a particular story that illustrates the power of **your** prayers. As kings and queens, we have great intercessory authority. When we walk into this anointing, we can see miracles happen through us, not just the priestly.

How about Abraham, the father of our faith, a kingly man of God? Remember the story of Abraham's intercession for Lot in Genesis 18:22-23. It took over eleven verses to record this businessperson's intercession and negotiation with the Lord not to wipe out Sodom where Lot lived. God honored Abraham by removing Lot and his wife and daughter by sending angels to get Lot out of the city. I hope you can see that when a king or queen prays, God answers, and in this case with angels.

Moses' prayers for his people were answered on several occasions. Remember when God told Moses that He wanted to kill all of Israel and start a new tribe with Moses? Moses interceded and asked God not to kill the people. Remember the story where Aaron and Miriam grumbled against Moses? The Lord gave leprosy to Miriam, and Moses interceded on her behalf so that she might be healed. God honored his request.

How about Joshua, who prayed to make the sun stand still in Joshua 10:12-15? Joshua, who was a military man, not a seminary student, asked God to hold the sun so he could finish conquering the enemy. God heard a request of a king and honored it.

This list goes on and on about how God answers prayers of kings and queens. Look at the life of Jesus, a carpenter, not of the tribe of Levi but a Melchizedek kingly priest. Look at the New Testament: It is chock full of kings, fishermen, tax collectors and others having their prayers answered and seeing the miracles of God happening prior to Jesus' death.

Now I want to take you to a great story of intercession by a king who reigned over Israel, Hezekiah. To prepare the story a little bit, Hezekiah was the son of Ahab, a bad king. He was raised by the most ungodly of fathers. He became king at 25 years of age and immediately requested that the priests sanctify themselves and initiate religious reform for their nation (2 Chronicles 29-31). Shortly after these reforms, (doing the right things) King Sennacherib of Assyria threatens to destroy King Hezekiah's kingdom. Isn't that just like the Devil to attack right after starting a new business, and as one gets close to God or their kingly ministry? Here is where the story of King Hezekiah's intercession begins in Isaiah Chapter 37.

Sennacherib sent his field commander with a very threatening letter to King Hezekiah. Read below what this heathen king had to say to this godly king:

⁴The field commander said to them, "Tell Hezekiah, 'This is what the great king, the king of Assyria, says: On what are you basing this confidence of yours? ⁵You say you have strategy and military strength, but you speak only empty words. On whom are you depending, that you rebel against me? ⁶Look now, you are depending on Egypt, that splintered reed of a staff, which pierces a man's hand and wounds him if he leans on it! Such is Pharaoh king of Egypt to all who depend on him.

⁷"And if you say to me, 'We are depending on the Lord our God'—isn't he the one whose high places and altars Hezekiah removed, saying to Judah and Jerusalem, 'You must worship before this altar'?

⁸"'Come now, make a bargain with my master, the king of Assyria: I will give you two thousand horses—if you can put riders on them! ⁹How then can you repulse one officer of the least of my master's officials, even though you are depending on Egypt for chariots and horsemen? ¹⁰Furthermore, have I come to attack and destroy this land without the Lord? The Lord himself told me to march against this country and destroy it.' "(Isaiah 36:4-10)

The field commander was rough. When they asked him to speak in Aramaic instead of Hebrew, he said the following back to the people there.

¹²*But the commander replied, "Was it only to your master and you that my master sent me to say these things, and not to the men sitting on the wall, who, like you, will have to eat their own filth and drink their own urine?"*

¹³*Then the commander stood and called out in Hebrew, "Hear the words of the great king, the king of Assyria! *¹⁴*This is what the king says: Do not let Hezekiah deceive you. He cannot deliver you! *¹⁵*Do not let Hezekiah persuade you to trust in the Lord when he says, 'The Lord will surely deliver us; this city will not be given into the hand of the king of Assyria.'*

¹⁶*"Do not listen to Hezekiah. This is what the king of Assyria says: Make peace with me and come out to me. Then every one of you will eat from his own vine and fig tree and drink water from his own cistern, *¹⁷*until I come and take you to a land like your own—a land of grain and new wine, a land of bread and vineyards.*

[18]*"Do not let Hezekiah mislead you when he says, 'The Lord will deliver us.' Has the god of any nation ever delivered his land from the hand of the king of Assyria?* [19]*Where are the gods of Hamath and Arpad? Where are the gods of Sepharvaim? Have they rescued Samaria from my hand?* [20]*Who of all the gods of these countries has been able to save his land from me? How then can the Lord deliver Jerusalem from my hand?"*

[21]*But the people remained silent and said nothing in reply, because the king had commanded, "Do not answer him."* [22]*Then Eliakim son of Hilkiah the palace administrator, Shebna the secretary, and Joah son of Asaph the recorder went to Hezekiah, with their clothes torn, and told him what the field commander had said. (Isaiah 36:12-22)*

After this, these messengers went to King Hezekiah, and his first response was to go to the temple of the Lord. This man had God at the core of him. He then sent leaders to the prophet Isaiah. Isaiah told the king not to worry. No harm would come to him and that Sennacherib would be killed.

The field commander went back to Sennacherib the king of Assyria and found that the king was going to start to fight Egypt. It is interesting though that King Sennacherib sent a letter to King Hezekiah. This letter states that Sennacherib would be back to destroy Judah:

⁹Now Sennacherib received a report that Tirhakah, the Cushite king of Egypt, was marching out to fight against him. When he heard it, he sent messengers to Hezekiah with this word: ¹⁰"Say to Hezekiah king of Judah: Do not let the god you depend on deceive you when he says, 'Jerusalem will not be handed over to the king of Assyria.' ¹¹ Surely you have heard what the kings of Assyria have done to all the countries, destroying them completely. And will you be delivered? ¹²Did the gods of the nations that were destroyed by my forefathers deliver them-the gods of Gozan, Haran, Rezeph and the people of Eden who were in Tel Assar? ¹³Where is the king of Hamath, the king of Arpad, the king of the city of Sepharvaim, or of Hena or Ivvah?" (Isaiah 37:9-13)

Hezekiah received the letter from Sennacherib and went back to the temple and spread out this letter of Sennacherib's putting it before the Lord. Listen to this King's intercession for those under his sphere of influence in Isaiah 37:14-21:

Royal Intercession

[14]Hezekiah received the letter from the messengers and read it. Then he went up to the temple of the Lord and spread it out before the Lord. [15]And Hezekiah prayed to the Lord: [16]"O Lord Almighty, God of Israel, enthroned between the cherubim, you alone are God over all the kingdoms of the earth. You have made heaven and earth. [17]Give ear, O Lord , and hear; open your eyes, O Lord , and see; listen to all the words Sennacherib has sent to insult the living God.

[18]"It is true, O Lord, that the Assyrian kings have laid waste all these peoples and their lands. [19]They have thrown their gods into the fire and destroyed them, for they were not gods but only wood and stone, fashioned by human hands. [20]Now, O Lord our God, deliver us from his hand, so that all kingdoms on earth may know that you alone, O Lord, are God."

[21]Then Isaiah son of Amoz sent a message to Hezekiah: "This is what the Lord, the God of Israel, says: Because you have prayed to me concerning Sennacherib king of Assyria. (Isaiah 37:14-21)

Then Isaiah sends a messenger to King Hezekiah. In verse 21, "This is what the Lord God of Israel says:

Because you have prayed." Because this king prayed Isaiah gives a very lengthy prophetic word in verses 21-35 stating God Himself will protect the city of Jerusalem and not to worry.

So far, the story is great; the bad king waits to attack a godly king, a godly king prays for the people to be safe and the prophet reassures them that this safety is coming from God. However, look at the way God fulfills His word to this king's prayer:

36Then the angel of the Lord went out and put to death a hundred and eighty-five thousand men in the Assyrian camp. When the people got up the next morning—there were all the dead bodies! 37So Sennacherib king of Assyria broke camp and withdrew. He returned to Nineveh and stayed there. (Isaiah 37:36-37)

Because of this kings intercession God sent one—I repeat one—angel to wipe out one hundred and eighty five thousand of Assyria's army that defeated all these other nations. Wow! One angel wipes out an entire army. Sennacherib returns to Nineveh.

Then God deals with Sennacherib by using his own sons to kill him while he was worshiping his heathen god. Therefore, God comes through at the end and totally removes the threat of this enemy.

Why? Because one king prayed. Because one king (not a priest) prayed, a nation's history was changed. We are a part of the intercessors of God. We the kingly are a part of the plan of God to pray in the desires of God and the earth. We are a plan of God's on the earth. We are to intercede for family, friends, priests, businesses and world affairs. Praise God if the kingly receive their herald call to intercede because God hears them and will work through to tear down wickedness in high places. Remember we comprise 92 percent of the body of Christ. If we do our part, the power of intercession will change world history again.

I hope this inspires you to take your prayer ministry seriously. You have the ear of God. He harkens unto a king or queen's prayers. You are very important to the kingdom. It is not the priest alone who will pray in the coming of God and the salvation of nations, it is also the kings and queens of our God.

V

Practically Praying
By Dennis Doyle

hen you think about it, prayer is every-
thing. Prayer is where we share ourselves
with God, and more importantly, He
shares Himself with us. God loves to talk to us and enjoys
listening to us as well. Whether you are the hourly worker,
salary worker, the CEO or owner of the company, prayer is
critical.

It is in the closet of prayer that you receive His
presence, His words, His heart and often the direction you
need for the day. Imagine a plane or ship traveling without
checking the instruments. You are familiar, I am sure, with
the story of the *Titanic*, great plans but poor following of

directions. As kings and queens, you need daily direction for the part you play in the kingdom, at home, work and church.

Prayer allows us to come into the presence of God. He is there and that makes prayer great and fun! You know, sometimes he shares with us during prayer time and other times he just cleanses the world, the worries and hassles away. Then peace and perspective occurs and often direction comes to our hearts as well. Remember, *"God directs the hearts of the king wheresoever he wills" (Proverbs 21:1)*. It is a great idea as kings and queens that we pray and give God our hearts to direct.

This is daily prayer. I know you have been told by priests to pray. However, as I understand how critical my prayers are I encourage you to get with God daily. Why? Not to be religious or foolish, it is much more practical than that. It is to get instructions from God.

You can save so much wear and tear on your life if you submit your decisions daily. Remember, a bad decision one day can get you big time months or years later. My experience is that God gives me a little at a time. In my business and life it is the little daily "What should I do, Lord?" prayers that add up to a lifestyle of hearing God and trying my best to follow His directions.

So, let us get practical. When you seek God, first

make sure your heart is right. Let Him deal with you. Let Him show you your pride, lust, fear, envy, greed, hatred, or any other fleshly pattern you might have. Do not get haughty and believe you do not have any of these; we all do. God can point these out and help us remove them. However, ask God if there is anything in your heart that He needs to address. Then listen, repent and feel better. There is nothing better than a king or queen with a pure heart before the Living God ready to follow Him for the day.

Next, make sure you and your spouse are in unity. This is extremely important. Megan and I have learned repeatedly the value of our heart being one before we go into prayer for our business. When we are not hindered, then we can be a real prayer covering for all the kings and queens who work along side of us as well as the lost who need prayer.

So some of the next steps of prayer I will talk about apply more to owners of businesses. I believe however that any king or queen in any position of business can apply many of these principles.

Spiritual mapping of a business is also a great help in practically praying for a company and the people within it. Think through the history of the companies or the departments you worked in. Has there been ungodly behavior or attitudes? Have there been partners splitting, employees quitting in anger, the taking advantage of people, lying or stealing. If these problems have taken place, reconciliation of these issues whenever possible is most critical. Owning our own ungodly behavior and humbling ourselves to fellow coworkers, regardless of rank is critical for having spiritual breakthroughs in the work environment, a holy place of God. Pray through the issues that need prayer and work through the issues that need to be worked through.

I believe God has a redemptive purpose for every business. Knowing the history, aiming in prayer regularly, we can know His will for a company, a department, and simply how to better love those around us.

I believe God has a redemptive purpose for every business.

Next, to pray practically we need to involve others. In our journey, we have a mixture of employees who were Christians, church friends, and local and national intercessors. These prayer partners for your company, department and boss need to be mature and able to keep confidences. This is a holy place when you pray over the work environment and its people. You as a group can stand before God (well actually sit, stand around, be prostrated on the floor or whatever) and tear down the strongholds, release blessings, call forth God's will and God's spirit to fill a place.

If your prayer partners are not local, keep them up to date with current issues facing the business. Try to be consistent with the times and places that you meet. Over the years, Megan and I have met in different places. Sometimes we met at our home with our employees and friends to pray; sometimes the boardroom at the office was the place we chose for a session. The other times we would prayer walk the whole building, office by office, outside the whole thing. When you do this, God can sometimes show you things you would not understand otherwise. A great time to pray is when there is no one in the building. Of course, have permission to be in the building and the authority to go into places before you pray.

Depending on the size of the company or departments there could be many people you are praying for. Get organized and make lists of people so you know the area God has given you to pray for. Then divide and conquer or pray as a group for each so you can be effective. Do not be intimidated. You will be amazed at how many people you can cover in prayer within an hour or so.

Now hear again, confidentiality is critical. We at times had an *A* list of intercessors to whom we told everything as business owners and were less open to our broader group of prayer partners. Yet our focused prayer together is incredible.

Why do we do all this? I believe that practically and strategically praying over your realm of influence is critical to taking back the territory that God wants us to have as kings and queens of the earth. We only can declare God's sovereignty over our business or realms of influence. If we don't do it, who will? As kings and queens, we are put on the earth to pray, "Thy will be done on earth as it is in heaven." We want His perfect will on earth and diligent prayer moves us into that direction.

Megan and I have been doing this now for over seven years. We still meet weekly at our house and pray for our businesses. We pray for the un-churched and churched every week as we think we should. I personally pray for all those who directly report to me. I believe we should pray in all directions for those in authority over us in the company, for those along side of us in our company and for those who report to us in any way; also praying for those accounts we maintain is very important.

I believe it is our prayers that give me more opportunity to hear God for them and at times be nicer than my flesh by itself would be. This changes me, and I know that it affects the work environment. The more like Christ I am, the better it is for everybody, everywhere.

Prayer, especially practical prayer is the battle of the kings and queens in the workplace. Bringing light to the marketplace like New Testament kings is imperative. We have the light of the world to chase back the enemy. Pray for our businesses. When workplaces are doing God's will, then the kingdom advances wherever we are.

Remember, this is a battlefield, and once you start aligning your sphere of influence, whether business, or employment, with God you have a natural enemy. Satan is real. Be ready for hell to break loose to dismay you or confuse you. Remember Peter and the disciples were put in the boat by Jesus in Matthew 14. Jesus put them in, and the waves were rough, and they did not think that it was fun. God changed their perspective that night. When you get serious about praying for your sphere of influence expect resistance. Be grounded in the word and a local church. Have a pastor know what is going on with you and stay honest.

Our battle is for the hearts and minds of other kings and queens who need Jesus. Only we are close enough to catch these people in our sphere of influence. For a net to catch fish, it has to be in proximity of the fish. We are the net for the people in the market place and the lost are the fish. Prayer is our tactic to attach them to Him and if we are truly dangerous for God then we are lethal to the enemy's grip on people's souls.

These souls come into the kingdom and into their own kingly ministry through discipleship by us. We can see the world change one important soul at a time. We, yes, we can save the world or at least the pond we are given to fish in.

I trust this has given you some practical ideas in which to attack. Attack daily, attack as a group, attack specifically, attack when you cannot see results, then rejoice in the variety of bounties our God has for you. Take your kingly and queenly authority in your sphere of influence and take the kingdom by force, Prayer force.

VI

Why?

he question repeatedly in my head is why kings and priests? Why didn't God make us alike? Why the differences? This took me back to the very beginning of the creation. When God creates something living to reproduce, he creates a unit not an individual. When God created mammals, birds and reptiles, he created them male and female.

As a Christian counselor, I know well that there is great wisdom in God giving children both a dad and a mom. In general, terms, mom often provides much of the nurturing and the compassionate aspects that a child definitely needs. Dad typically lets children take more risk, rough houses with them and has a masculine approach to parenting that may appear less compassionate at times, but truly isn't.

As children grow, hopefully they take the best of their father and the best of their mother and balance the truths, principles and attitudes that they heard and experienced from both parents. A child with a godly father and mother can become more balanced than if they had just been raised by one parent.

What does all this parenting stuff have to do with kings and queens? I think quite a bit. Parents are a great way to explain the value of our role in the body of Christ and to grasp that we must honor the role of the priest.

In my journey as a Christian, I have been trained as a priest and a king. I have been privileged to be in kingly and priestly meetings locally and nationwide. As a Christian counselor, I have worked with many kings and priests. I say this to state that I have no ax to grind. I love kings and queens and I love priests, but they are often as different as night and day. Both need to understand each other and honor each other if the children of God in the local body of Christ are to grow up balanced and strong.

When I am around kings and queens, I am amazed at how thorough their thinking process is. They tend to have a way about them that has no real need to be liked but rather a need to solve a problem. Put ten kings in a room and aim at a problem and it will be an interesting process to watch. It is like watching hungry wolves devour a prey. They can make lists, come up with practical angles and have even the largest problem solved quickly. Then they are quick to assign responsibilities and put in place measurable goals and measurable outcomes to see if the problems are solved.

The weakness of kings and queens is they can easily and effectively solve a problem but often to the neglect of relational realities. How will a person feel about this or what are the effects on the families who are taking the action points are not often considered by the kingly. The just get it done motif is popular with the kingly types.

Priests, however, are different; they can spend hours discussing the same issue and will look primarily at the relational aspects. How will so-and-so feel and how does this affect their family? They may get to the same place as kings but they are processing is so different.

One major difference is the way kings and queens and priests think about paying for their great kingdom ideas. The kings I have met will generally pay for their great ideas themselves. If they cannot financially afford the project themselves, they are apt to go ask a few other kings or queens to help to get the funding for it. Kings and queens rarely think in terms of committees. They think in terms of the shortest path between two points.

As kings and queens, we see mandates from God as our personal responsibility, not the responsibility of others.

Kings and queens rarely mind paying for what they believe is their ministry responsibility on the earth. As kings and queens, we see mandates from God as our personal responsibility, not the responsibility of others.

Priests, however, will come up with the very same great ideas. They will have many meetings to affirm the idea is either good or from God. They will then develop methods or opportunities to have a group of others pay for the idea.

Now in balance I think it is reasonable and responsible for priests to know they are hearing from God and receiving counsel in the decision making process. After all, they are handling holy money that was laid at the feet of our God through tithes and offerings.

Another answer to the question as to why both kings and priests, is for balance. In writing this book, I have talked to both kings and priests about the paradigms we have covered throughout the book. What is interesting are the different responses that kings, queens, and priests had. Both regularly seem to respond from a place of hurt from the other. The kings and queens felt hurt because they felt they were only good for the money they provided to the church. Some kings and queens did not feel the priests (pastor, pastoral staff, etc.) affirmed their calling to a non-traditional ministry. They felt that they were misunderstood and were not good enough to function in a leadership role nor asked for input in areas they are thought to be proficient in.

On the other hand, priests shared with me their issues of being hurt from the kings and queens in their congregation. Priest after priest told me countless stories of how kings came on like gangbusters, making all kinds of resource promises only not to follow through repeatedly. They would share how kings and queens would want to be "obeyed" rather than be a team player. Priest would report how an elder, deacon or board of directors would be callous to the needs of people in need, and want the pastor to preach or not to preach on certain topics.

You can see how a misunderstanding or failure to honor each other can lead to significant pain. Like a marriage when one role, position or person is elevated too greatly above the other causes all kinds of dysfunction and pain. The games, power plays and manipulation of each other can lead to an erosion or destruction of a marriage.

I believe kings and queens and priests are to honor and balance each other. Together we are made in His image. We both hold aspects of the nature and heart of God that the other does not intuitively possess.

The married couple who learns early on that Christ through each of them will get them closer to understanding His heart, nature and will is both fortunate and balanced. The situation where one person hears from God and the other is made to feel less spiritual does not work and is dishonoring to our God.

Like a marriage when one role, position or person is elevated too greatly above the other causes all kinds of dysfunction and pain.

If you can imagine the balance of a good marriage, then you can see why God designed kings and priests. They are two distinct roles that, when combined, can enable the pair to hear from God, raise godly offspring and most importantly, model unity to the body of Christ.

If you can imagine a church leadership team that combines the priestly leaders and kingly leaders to hear from God, then you can truly imagine what is God's heart for the next generation of His church. Imagine a city leadership of local pastors and local businesspeople seeking God through prayer and fasting, finding His will and accomplishing it together. Imagine the love of God they would have for each other and the mutual respect as they both accomplish together what neither could do individually.

Now take that to a state or national level. I truly believe we would need less government if kings and priests would team up, love each other, accept their differences and do the will of the Father together. The Father's heart is one of unity. Jesus prayed that we would be one even as He and the Father are one (John 17:21).

God gave us the marriage analogy to illustrate to us how two different types of His expression can become one. As a married man I know the longer I am married to my wife Lisa, the more we become like each other. This oneness as kings and priests can create so much of the kingdom of God on the earth.

Think of a city crusade where not only pastors speak, but electricians, business leaders and anointed kings and queens speak and see miracles happen. Can you imagine kings and queens who seek out priests to hear their ideas, be affirmed and know that they are prayed for? If you can imagine this then you are definitely part of the solution of seeing balance brought together in the body of Christ.

Ministry of Kings and Queens

As kings and queens, whether you are a line worker, a business owner or service professional or stay at home mother, you can lead in the move toward balance. Encourage the priestly ministers in your life. Tell them what they are doing **right**. Sow the fruits of kindness and love toward them. Empower their vision and above all protect them. They are God's people just as we are, equal but different.

I think kings and queens can lead the way to unity. You have influence to encourage the priest. Invite them to your meetings if you want them to invite you to theirs. Let them know they are on your formal or informal advisory committee. They might not know your business, but priests know God and can see things you might be missing.

It works both ways. It is not about us as kings and queens being able to express our ministry, but rather allowing priests to share their ministry in your world. In this way, we send a loud message to the priest and to the lost.

I have heard many kings and queens complain that their pastor does not care about their business or place of work. Then I ask them when the last time was that they invited their pastor to visit their business or place of work. Have you asked your pastor to pray over where you work? Introduce him to people with whom you interact. What a message the world would see of how important spiritual things and Christ is to you if your pastor is honored regularly to sit in on a meeting, to pray over a group for wisdom and seek God's will.

Most priests are honored to come to your place of business. This sends the message that they are an important part of your team.

So ask yourself, "Am I a king or queen doing what I need to do to make my priestly ministers feel a part of my world and my business?" If the answer is no, start here. Invite your pastor to pray over your business, or hold an official dedication of your business to the Lord. Pick your pastor up and bring him to a meeting or two or lunch. Invite your pastor to go out to lunch with the gang. That would give the staff at the office something to talk about. Later, when storms hit your coworkers' or employees' lives, they will already know Pastor Joe and feel more comfortable talking to him. After all, they have eaten together four times in the last year.

You see, if you empower the priestly ministers in your life, then they can respect your world and hear the prayer needs in your business. Then when you have a ministry idea, it will be heard in a relational context and possibly be more likely to be received. As kings and queens if we do the relationship building work first, we can really facilitate unity between us. We need each other, and when we are together, more can be done.

So if you are a king or queen who has complained about the priestly, get them involved in your sphere of influence. Then you have a place to be heard by example in their sphere of influence.

There is another reason why the kings and priests combined vision is so important for the body of Christ is to operate optimally and take dominion of the earth through the gospel.

Again, I have to go to an analogy to make my point. Often kings and queens have been taught that the priest provides the vision and kings the provision. I think this is not exactly balanced. In the Old Testament, on more than one occasion, the king provided vision.

When King Hezekiah told the priests to sanctify themselves, they would be reminded of the Word of God. The priests provided spiritual leadership and vision. Who can argue that the Father of our faith did not have spiritual vision or David or Joseph, etc.? Kings and queens often have both vision and provision. We are not laborers who only provide
resources; we are laborers in the kingdom fully, spiritually, emotionally and financially and we are as "anointed" as any of our priestly collaborators.

I believe that both kings and queens and priests

have vision. My experience leads me to a generalization about the sphere of vision which both primarily see.

To illustrate this I must go back to husband and wife roles that God ordained. All of us who are married are different from our spouses. We come that way from birth because God decides our gender. Our genders not only affect our various roles in marriage but also the way we process and see life based on our perspective.

I truly believe we would need less government if kings and priests would team up.

In my house as the husband/father/counselor, I believe I am sensitive, can talk about intimacy and actually lead in these areas with my wife as Christ does with the church. I am often amazed at our life together and how intuitively natural that intimacy occurs.

However, with our children, Lisa has an uncanny gift of discernment. She supernaturally (to my male mind) knows what to do when they are sick. She has a vigorous commitment to their development, especially when it comes to school, music and activities. She amazes me with how much vision she has for our kids in these and other areas. Maternal instincts provide vision for the children and their surroundings. The point is my wife has vision for the kids, the household and relationships. I call this "inside the house" vision.

On the other side, although I am involved with these processes, I often do not "see it" first. My vision is more "outside of the house." My vision comprises books to write and different ways to advance an aspect of the kingdom of God. My priorities include loving my family, protecting them and planning our finances. Maintaining and acting on a vision for their financial future, as well as encouraging my children and seeing them take risks and grow, is intuitive and easy for my masculine soul. My vision encompasses mostly outer vision.

Both the outer vision and inner vision are important. Although there is some small overlapping in Lisa's and my vision, largely they are complementing visions.

This explains my experience when I am around kings or queens. They often are concerned with the unreached in their city, the less fortunate and missions like constructing a church in another country. The kings and queens I know want to build orphanages, minister to the inner city or bless mission work and are quick to see a ministry that may be needed in the church if it is not there. Like one king, I know who saw a lack of outreach to the youth donated funding so his church could create a youth budget.

Kings and queens are visionaries as well. Often priests intuitively have vision for the members of the local church. They know what the people need. They intuitively know what they need to be educated, the areas of development they need and how they themselves are to exercise their spiritual gifts. They do this intuitively and with great anointing from God.

It amazes me how God will use them to speak the exact Word of God to kings and queens. All of us have received life-giving words from our priests, both men and women of God. These words of life, encouragement and connection are priceless. Their intuition after looking you in the eyes and asking, "Are you okay?" when you are struggling with sin, a decision or relationship is very uncanny. Kind of the way a mom knows when something is up with her children, so a good priestly pastor knows when a king or queen is disturbed: It is God-given intuition. All kings and queens should respect the way priests feed, plan for development and encourage. Priests have primarily inside vision for the house.

Can you see it if kings and priests operate the mystery of marriage rather than rival over power? Salvation and miracles can happen all over the world. The kings and priests do not interrelate at this intimate level in most

89

churches, but they can.

Truly, I think most priests know as little about kings as kings and queens know about priests. We are not to be totally like each other but rather to accept each other as a gift of God to each other. I truly know that without Lisa, my life would be less effective and much less fulfilling than it is with her. Too often we kings, queens, and priests act like couples that do not get along and do not know why God put us together.

Therefore, I believe that the vision of both kings and queens and priests are absolutely vital for a healthy body of Christ. Both need to be actively pursuing their vision while being supported by each other. As a team, they do much more together than either could do independently.

Kings and queens need to embrace our outside vision and work together for the inside vision of the house as well. How does this work? We should be faithful, dependable, active members of our church and supporters of the vision of our church. Let your pastor know you are praying for him. Encourage him as his aspirations material-ize.

Ask what you need to do to get your vision to manifest in the way God had uniquely designed you. As a king or queen, your vision may be somewhat nontraditional. However, if you involve your pastor along the way, both of you can rejoice when the goals you have envisioned happen.

Together we will accomplish more, reach more people and glorify God, who in His divine wisdom married us until death do us part. I encourage you as kings and queens to make it the absolute best marriage you can. Step up to plate, it only takes one spouse to start a chain reaction of change in a marriage. Lead in unity and all of God's family will be better off for generations

VII

Rebuilding the Walls

he paradigm of kings and priests working together to accomplish God's will on earth clearly illustrated in the rebuilding of the walls in Nehemiah 3. Before getting to the center of this picture of kingly and priestly unity, we have to address some of the background briefly so we can understand the context.

Nehemiah was a cupbearer to the King Artaxerxes, a heathen king. When Nehemiah's brother Hanani visited him from Judah, he inquired about Jerusalem. Hanani reported the exiles were in bad shape and the city's walls were broken down. Note that Nehemiah was a government employee to a heathen king. He was not a priest.

Nehemiah was deeply troubled about those in Jerusalem. I think this is so incredible. He was living and working in a great palace. He was probably wearing the best designer clothes of his day; after all, the king had to look at him regularly. He was eating in the palace daily. This was a great job, a great life, comfortable and full of benefits. How many Jews at this time could say they even saw the king? Nehemiah not only saw the king, he knew the king personally to some degree. How many hundreds or even thousands of hours had he observed the king's conversations, mannerisms, moods and preferences? Yet his heart ached for his fellow Jews in his homeland.

Most of these Jews were not even related to Nehemiah; they were simply members of the same spiritual family. Nehemiah had a heart for God's people, not just for his own life. Look in Nehemiah 1 and see how this kingly government employee sought God through days of weeping, prayer, intercession and fasting. He ached so much it changed his life priorities to the point of focusing on others. Let us read this kingly minister's prayer:

4When I heard these things, I sat down and wept. For some days I mourned and fasted and prayed before the God of heaven. 5Then I said: "O Lord, God of heaven,

94

the great and awesome God, who keeps his covenant of love with those who love him and obey his commands, ⁶let your ear be attentive and your eyes open to hear the prayer your servant is praying before you day and night for your servants, the people of Israel. I confess the sins we Israelites, including myself and my father's house, have committed against you. ⁷We have acted very wickedly toward you. We have not obeyed the commands, decrees and laws you gave your servant Moses.

⁸"Remember the instruction you gave your servant Moses, saying, 'If you are unfaithful, I will scatter you among the nations, ⁹but if you return to me and obey my commands, then even if your exiled people are at the farthest horizon, I will gather them from there and bring them to the place I have chosen as a dwelling for my Name.'

¹⁰"They are your servants and your people, whom you redeemed by your great strength and your mighty hand. ¹¹O Lord, let your ear be attentive to the prayer of this your servant and to the prayer of your servants who delight in revering your name. Give your servant success today by granting him favor in the presence of this man."

I was cupbearer to the king. (Nehemiah 1:4-11)

What I love about his prayer is he truly played the role of the intercessor. Nehemiah knew God's Word. It was embedded in his heart. He brought God's Word to God the Father. He identified himself with being a sinner like the people of God. He asked for favor not for himself but so others could be helped.

I love kings and queens who pray. When we pray for others like Jesus did and still does, God moves. This man's prayers changed world history. Think about it: Maybe you have a job or business and you think, "I am not helping much or doing much for God." Nehemiah is a great example of how to change that and be an instrumental part in changing your city for the better. We kings and queens can change world history! Our prayers and intercessions are valid.

A king's or queen's particular focus represents his part of the wall.

Back to Nehemiah: Sadness for Jerusalem engulfed him and captured the heathen king's attention. When the king asks Nehemiah about it, he told Artaxerxes how the walls of his family's city had been destroyed and left in disrepair. Therefore, Artaxerxes released Nehemiah to go and rebuild the walls. Nehemiah also requested safe travel letters to his homeland and a letter to receive timber. God granted Nehemiah supernatural protection and provision to accomplish his kingly ministry.

Therefore, Nehemiah goes to Jerusalem. He inspects the city and motivates the local people to start rebuilding the walls of Jerusalem. Although Nehemiah experienced long-term resistance from Sanballat and Tobiah, he prevailed. I say this because kingly ministry may meet with resistance, but the resistance will not prevail; it is just a nuisance during the process.

In chapter 3 of Nehemiah, we see hands-on people who tackle their kingly, queenly, and priestly ministry to see the walls rebuilt. As you go through the list of people that day in and day out toiled in this work, it is interesting to note how the Bible identifies them. Some of these people are priests and Levites, but most are government workers, jewelry makers, and from all other walks of life. Now realize every one of the hundreds or thousands that may have helped rebuild the walls is not listed in the Book of Nehemiah; rather it describes each person who was in charge of a group and assigned to a certain sector of the wall.

I find this often in kingly ministry. A king's or

queens's particular focus represents his part of the wall. He or she is not motivated to participate with other parts of the wall. It is as if God gives kings or queens eyes, ears and a heart for a certain aspect of the city and that is where they camp to rebuild. That can be frustrating for priests or other kings who want them to use their giftedness for a different part of the wall. I would encourage you to find your niche and be obedient, but also be kind to those who have other placements along the wall.

I find chapter 3 of Nehemiah to be a very interesting chapter. Nehemiah is listing the people rebuilding the walls in three major categories: priest, Levites and others. The others are those whom I call the kings and queens. These are the men and women with daily responsibilities at work or home but make the time to do God's work for the betterment of all.

As you read chapter 3 you will find Elishib the high priest and his fellow priests, who worked on the Sheep Gate (verse 1). Verse 17 mentions another priest and a group of Levites who worked near the House of the Heroes. In verse 22, we see Levite priests from the surrounding areas working on a part of the wall next to Eliashib's house. Then verse 28 tells of priests making repairs in front of their own houses next to the Horse Gate.

Therefore, in this wall project we have four priestly

groups doing their part. I think this is great. These Levites were trying to take care of their other responsibilities with their families. I am glad that Nehemiah highlighted these hard working priests. These four groups made a real contribution to the wall.

Nehemiah, however, does not stop there. There are almost forty kingly ministries working hard as well. These groups of men and women also made their contributions proportionately. It is interesting to note how Nehemiah identifies the people who give of their lives to accomplish their kingly and queenly ministry to rebuild their city. I am going to list the verse, the section of the wall and how Nehemiah identifies these ancient kingly ministers.

Verse	Part of the Wall	Kingly Ministers
3:2	Adjoining section	Men of Jericho
	Next Section	Zaccur son of Imri
3:3	Fish gate	Sons of Hassenaah
3:4	Next Section	Meremoth son of Uriah
	Next Section	Meshullam son of Berekiah

	Next Section	Zadak son of Baana
3:5	Next Section	Men of Tekoa
3:6	Jeshanah Gate	Joiada son of Paseah and Meshullam son of Besodeiah
3:7	Next Section	Melatiah of Gibeon and Jadon of Meronoth in Mizpah
3:8	Next Section up to the Broad Wall	Uzziel, a goldsmith
	Next Section up to the Broad Wall	Hananiah, a perfume maker
3:9	Next Section	Rephaiah, ruler a half-district in Jerusalem
3:10	Next Section	Jedaiah son of

		Harumaph
	Next Section	Hattush son of
		Hashabneiah
3:11	Next section and the	Malkijah son of
	Tower of Ovens	Harim Hasshub
		son of Pahath-
		Moab
3:12	Next Section	Shallum, ruler a
		half-district of
		Jerusalem, and
		his daughters
3:13	Valley Gate and wall up to	Hanun and resi-
	the Dung Gate	dents of Zanoah
3:14	Dung Gate	Malkijah, ruler of
		Beth Hakkerem
		district
3:15	Fountain Gate and Pool of	Shallun, ruler of
	Siloman's well	Mizpah
		district
3:16	Next Section	Nehemiah, ruler a

		half-district of Beth Zur
3:17	Next Section	Hashabiah, ruler of a half-district of Keilah
3:18	Next Section	Countrymen under Binnui, ruler of a half-district of Keilah
3:19	Next Section	Ezer, ruler of Mizpah
3:20	Next Section	Baruch son of Zabbai
3:21	Next Section	Meremoth son of Uriah
3:23	Next Section	Benjamin and Hasshub
	Next Section	Azariah son of Maseiah

3:24	Next Section	Binnui son of Henadad
3:25	Next Section	Palal son of Uzai
3:26	Next Section up to the projecting tower	Pedaiah son of Parosh and temple servants
3:27	From projecting tower to wall of Ophel	Men of Tekoa
3:29	Next Section	Zadok son of Immer
	Next Section	Shemaiah son of Shecaniah
3:30	Next Section	Hananiah son of Shelemiah and Hanun sixth son of Zalaph
	Next Section	Meshullam son of Berekiah
3:31	Next Section	Malkijah, a gold

3:32   Next Section   Goldsmiths and

merchants

This is a very long list of kingly types. Over 37 major people are identified, and many had groups of people helping them. I wanted you to see the list because I think it is probably the best single picture of not only the priestly and kingly working together but also of the kingly and kingly working together.

The people who worked on the wall had several titles: rulers, countrymen, men or residents of a location, merchants, goldsmiths, perfume makers and daughters. These business owners, skilled labor, women and untold hundreds of others were focused on their part of the rebuilding project while maintaining a sense of the bigger picture.

This is kingly ministry at its best: employees and employers, government workers, skilled laborers, men and women with hearts for a certain ministry working and focused together with each other and the priests. Together walls are rebuilt and cities are put back together.

I know you are thinking that there are no men with horses and spears trying to tear down the city you live in.

Our battles are much different: fatherlessness, pornography, teen pregnancy, abortion, poverty and welfare to name a few.

To solve the largest issues facing our cities will take all of us in the body of Christ. The priests cannot do it alone and neither can the kings and queens. Solutions will only come by accepting each other for who we are and not lusting after each other's abilities or roles. We should receive our position on the wall with a group of people and focus on rebuilding our cities.

The job of Nehemiah was not to build the temple. He was a government employee sent on pretty much a social project. If kings and priests are to change our culture and influence for the kingdom of God, we must allow people to be themselves and work on the part of the wall for which they have a heart and vision.

Each of us as kings and queens has a part on the wall. In general terms our role is to love, protect and minister to others from various arenas of life. For some, our ministry is social. God may touch our hearts to give or volunteer at the Salvation Army, a women's shelter, a teen addiction center, juvenile homes, pregnancy centers, etc. For others our workplace is our kingly or queenly ministry. For some the ministry is supportive of the local church or para-church ministry. Whatever your calling, go for it! You are able to touch and love people wherever the Lord has planted you. But whatever you do, do something. God has not called one kingly minister to the pew ministry. If all you do for Jesus is go to church and give money, you would be throwing off your responsibility to rebuild the wall. Remember David got in trouble when he stayed home from war. Evaluate your kingly ministry if you are not touching somebody for Jesus you are behaving like laity, not as the royalty the blood of Jesus made you to be.

Nehemiah provides a great outline for birthing kingly ministry on the earth. Firstly, Nehemiah was faithful on his present job. He did not just become extremely angry. He showed up for work day after day. Even though his duty as a cupbearer was not one of the more impressive in the palace, he must have maintained a positive attitude for the king to notice the change in his countenance. Therefore, principle number one on birthing a kingly ministry is to be faithful and have a good attitude on your current job.

The next thing we see is heartfelt prayer. Nehemiah identified himself before God with the pains of God's people. He knew God's heart and God's Word. He truly bathed the situation at hand in prayer. The second principle is intercessory prayer and an indwelling of God's Word in your life.

After praying about it, Nehemiah must have done

some homework. He must have looked at a map to see which people groups would let him pass through their land. He thought through the need for wood and knew the top man to deal with to obtain the wood. Nehemiah took time to consider the practical aspects of rebuilding the wall. Principle number three, then, is to sit down with paper and pen and write out the practical aspects that apply to your ministry calling. If it's a building you need, figure out the costs and proper zoning, shop the market, set salaries for employees, know the tax laws, and so on. Whatever the ministry—social, medical, media, para-church or local church—get practical.

Research what others have already done in this area of ministry. So much time in the kingdom is reinventing the same wheel repeatedly. Decide if this is an abundance ministry you are funding or a nonprofit organization. How will it start to create self-sustaining revenue? I know it is not all spiritual to think this way but this is important if your kingly ministry is going to be birthed. Principle number four is get practical and get your facts straight before starting.

The next step Nehemiah presents in his situation is finding a person who can actually do something about it. I find it interesting that this was a heathen king, not a religious group. This was a kingly talking to a heathen king. Sometimes it may be as valuable to talk to a few businesspersons, as it is to discuss an issue with church staffers. Regardless of whom you meet with, make sure you are talking to someone who can actually help you get things done. That is principle number five: Talk to movers and shakers in your area of ministry that can help you get the job done for the kingdom of God.

The Nehemiah we see is a man of follow-through and motivation of others. He shows up in town, lays out the vision and gets started. He is a persistent kingly minister and works hard getting this large task accomplished. Follow-through and the ability to inspire is definitely the next principle for birthing kingly ministry.

The following step is taking counsel in the Lord and godly advisors. Nehemiah knew God and God's heart for this ministry of rebuilding the walls. When the neighbors did not like what was going on, they spread lies about Nehemiah. They repeatedly tested the man of God. They wanted him to become afraid and discouraged. Nehemiah would have no part of their demonic tactics. He stayed focused, responding to attacks practically, but never stopping. He sought God and stayed focused even under pressure. Principle number seven is, seek God and stay focused.

The last principle is to stay humble and enjoy the Lord's deliverance. Nehemiah never took on an air of haughtiness. I think humility is an earmark of those who see a ministry from birth to success.

I hope these principles can help birth, pray through, practically prepare, involve the right people, go through the fire and see God as a delivering and compassionate God about your kingly ministry. I encourage you to find your place on the wall and advance the kingdom. Frustrate the Devil and change the world.

Take a minute and take a tablet of paper, write down what you would do for the kingdom of God or your city if you absolutely knew you could not fail. What are the dreams or abilities God has given you. Now that you know that you are absolutely a king or queen of God that is not only royal but also responsible, what are you to do?

Get silent before the Lord and ask, Lord what would you have this servant do. Petition Christ until He responds and then follow out of the comfortable boat into His glorious ministry for you. The world and church is waiting for you to rise up and fulfill your part of the wall.

VIII

Work Theology
By Dennis Doyle

In the Beginning…

 hen God created the world (according to the Book of Genesis), He delighted in all that He had created. We can read after each created work, "and God saw that it was good." By the sixth day, in Genesis 1:31, we read, "Then God saw everything that He had made, and indeed it was VERY good."

Throughout all of Scripture, the very essence of truth or efforts to align with truth are defined by whether or not God is pleased and considers the idea "good." Before the fall, all of creation pleased the Father. After the fall, the world toiled in agony to be reconciled—but there was no man, no sacrifice worthy to reconcile them. In the fullness of time, the world was reconciled to God once again through His Son, Jesus Christ. To those who seek the Lord through His Son, His will and pleasure are once again revealed.

During our recent years of travel and conference speaking, my wife and I have met businesspeople from all over the world. In this chapter, we would like to address some of the comments we have heard through the years. Comments like:

⊙ "I believed that working hard and producing wealth wasn't godly and that we might be somewhat greedy or manipulative for storing up wealth for ourselves." (Or in other words, WEALTH = GREED and MANIPU-LATION).

⊙ "I thought that mankind was made solely for a relationship with God and that work was part of the fall. I thought work was a punishment for the sin that entered the world."

⊙ "I felt that work was inconsequential to God. I thought it was more important to be in full-time ministry than it was to work at a job."

⊙ "I always believed that heaven was a place where we

wouldn't work. Isn't heaven a place where we sit around on clouds relaxing all day with harps and beautiful music playing?"

⊙ "Isn't retirement my reward for hard work? I always thought I should work a certain number of years and then, after saving enough money, retire and go and do whatever I want."

Christian businesspeople everywhere are whole-heartedly seeking to please God in their lives. In addition to the above listed misconceptions, many Christian businesspeople are confused and perplexed about their role in the body of Christ. They desire to be used by God in a significant way, but are disappointed that after a packed week working at their business, they do not have the time or energy to be greatly involved at their local church.

This frustration, for the most part, seems to originate with the confused idea that in order to be used by God; we must develop a position of ministry within the local church. Do not misunderstand me; ministry within the local church is valid and necessary on every level. This message does not exclude that fact. On the contrary, the good news we would like to declare to the multitude of Christian businesspeople that are frustrated and perplexed is; **God wants to use you mightily right now—right where you**

are—in the marketplace. God wants to reveal His plans and purposes to you by revealing the purposes of the kingdom that are fulfilled through your leadership in business.

God has a specific and redemptive call upon your life, your family and your business. It is up to you to discover it and allow God's kingdom plans to be revealed on earth as it is in heaven. It is not so much what **we** can do, but what **He** can do through us if we allow Him. We are God's instruments of redemption to this world.

Are you saying that God wants to use me for kingdom purposes at my job? Are you saying God has an eternal plan for me to fulfill in my work?

Yes, God who created the idea of work and occupations. In addition, according to God, that plan is **VERY** good.

The Concept of Work

In order to understand the role of a businessperson in kingdom purposes, let us begin by investigating God's opinion on the subject. What does God think about the concept of work? One way to study a word or concept in Scripture is to apply the rule of first mention.

Scholars throughout the ages have studied Scriptures using this method. The idea is to examine God's original intent for a given word or concept by studying the Scripture reference where it is first mentioned. A few of the questions we seek to answer are: How did God first intend the concept of work to be understood? What is the biblical concept of work? How did the concept of work originate?

I would also like to guide you through a word study of the word "work," starting with its first usage in Genesis 2:2-3 and ending with Genesis 5:29. This word study will give us a good overview of God's purpose and meaning for "work."

*²By the seventh day God had finished the **work** he had been doing; so on the seventh day He rested from all His **work**. ³And God blessed the seventh day and made it holy, because on it He **rested** from all the **work** of creating that He had done.*

These two verses of Scripture not only establish the first mention of work—they also help us to discover the priority that God places upon work. We recognize this in that work was literally the first action of creation. With this discovery, we can conclude that work (implemented in the very creation of the world—God's idea of perfection) is a good thing.

The Book of Genesis is a very foundational book in the Bible—particularly the first three and a half chapters. In these chapters, God reveals how the world was originally created and we can literally capture a glimpse of how He intended the earth to be.

God was thinking about man and his work even before man was created.

This portion of Scripture also gives us an overview of God's idea of perfection upon the earth before the fall of man. The rest of Scripture is a depiction of humankind's struggles after the fall, combined with messages of hope and God's plan to redeem the world from the ravages of sin, and the glorious fulfillment of that plan through His Son, Jesus.

The very idea that God clearly defines work so thoroughly during these first three chapters of the Bible is very significant in understanding our role in the kingdom of God today.

God Worked

The first person to develop the concept of work (by working himself) was God! In fact, the very first Scripture of the Bible records God working. God considered the act of "creating the earth" work. Genesis 1:1 says, *"In the beginning, God created the heavens and the earth."* Creation was the first act of God recorded in the Bible, and God called creation "work."

The literal second mention of work is found in Genesis 2:5: *"And no shrub of the field had yet appeared on the earth and no plant of the field had yet sprung up, for the Lord God had not sent rain on the earth and there was no man to **work** the ground."*

This verse tells us two important things. First, it develops the very concept of work. It describes God's need for someone to work the ground. Secondly, it introduces the concept that God ordained for man to pick up where He left off. God created the ground, but He wanted man to work and manage that ground.

In other words, creation would not be complete without man to accomplish God's intentions of working the ground. In fact, that work is God ordained from the beginning of time. This portrays to us how man and work were intrinsically interconnected. Man simply cannot find fulfillment on earth apart from the work he was created to do.

It is also intriguing to note that God was thinking about man and his work even before man was created.

Man is mentioned here in the midst of the creation of the world—"for the Lord God had not sent rain on the earth and there was no man to work the ground." Therefore, man was created with a distinct relationship to work. From the beginning, God created the earth with the intent that it should be managed and maintained by man.

Today, the plan is the same. God provides us with careers as part of our life in Him. He carefully postures us with life skills, gifts and talents in order that we would do works of service for His glory in the field of work He has placed us in. Work is a critical part of our life in Christ. So important is our work on the earth, that without it, we would not fulfill our destiny and God cannot fulfill His plans for the earth.

In our conversations with people from the business community, we too often hear confusion in their voices as they compare their work in business to the perceived greater importance of people work in fulltime ministry. This inaccurate comparison is rooted in the misconception that the work of God is only done within the traditional church.

Our goal is to educate and inform the body of Christ with regard to the value and priority that God himself places upon work in general and upon the people called by God in the marketplace. We must never allow anyone to tell us that our work is not important because according to

118

His Word, God himself created work for humankind.

Getting to the Root

Let us take an even closer look at the word "work." There are over one thousand mentions of the word "work" in the Old Testament alone.

To continue our study, let us focusing on three predominant meanings for "work" found in the Book of Genesis:

⊙   *Malak*—To occupy our time with a skill or occupation

⊙   *Abad*—To till the ground. To tend in our profession

⊙   *Shamar*—To keep watch or guard and protect

The first predominant meaning comes from the Hebrew word *malak,* which is the root of *malacah,* meaning occupy, occupation, work or business.

Genesis 2:2-3 uses this word when explaining that on the seventh day, God rested from his work (*malak*).

Malacah is used 130 times in Old Testament Scriptures. In contrast to the physical aspect of work, this word emphasizes skills and benefits. It is used to refer to work within one's occupation or in the area of governing and managing the affairs of man.

Exodus 30:1-3, *malacah* refers to God using supernatural skills for the work or partisanship of the Tabernacle. This use of the word occupation or "work" also places its emphasis on skills and occupation. God specifically gifted artisans to create the tabernacle. Today God bestows skills upon us for specific occupations so that we can serve Him in a very practical way here on earth.

This idea of occupying our time with our skills and talents is very important for us to understand in order to obey the command of Jesus to "occupy until I come." In Luke 19:11-27, Jesus speaks a parable of the *minas*. The command given to the servant was to occupy or "to do business" until I come. This word occupy literally implies "a fulfillment or completion of the work." We must work (occupy) our time in daily relationship with the Lord and complete the work that God started.

Another meaning for "work" is from the Hebrew root word *abad,* which means to cultivate, to till, to labor or serve. More than the all-encompassing idea of occupying—using our skills and talents—this word is very hands on in action.

In Genesis 2:5, God establishes the idea that He intended for man to cultivate and till the ground in the garden. It was up to man to determine the condition of the ground. While man was in perfect fellowship with God, this task of taking care of the ground and being a steward of all God had made was a blessing to him. It was the contamination of sin that made the task toilsome and heavy for him to bear.

This word *abad* or *cultivate* is related to another word with the same root—culture. Again, in the same way, the one who cultivates determines the condition of our very culture. As we take care of working *abad* God's creation, we cultivate and create the culture of the world we live in.

Here is an interesting theory to consider. According to Scripture, before the fall Adam and Eve were in a "heaven-type" garden and in perfect relationship with God. Every need was satisfied, yet God had work for them to do. Were Adam and Eve experiencing heaven on earth?

Perhaps you imagine heaven as it is depicted in Hollywood—people floating around on puffy clouds with harps and halos. The truth is, throughout Scripture heaven is described as a place where we, the redeemed, will actually rule and reign with Christ. Regardless of what form this role will take in its actuality, it is clear we will have an active part to play—ruling and reigning (working) with Christ.

Finally, a third meaning for "work" comes from the Hebrew word, *shamar,* meaning "to guard and protect, to be a watchman, to watch closely."

Then the Lord God took the man and put him in the Garden of Eden to tend (abad) *and keep* (shammar) *it. (Genesis 2:15)*

God was literally asking Adam to guard and protect the garden, to be CEO over the earth. As a guard, the idea is to walk around, observe, understand and react to threats.

This aspect of work is also important to note as it connotates the idea of "overseer" of a territory. This is a very important aspect of work as it calls us to responsibility of authority; to bring oversight and leadership to our sphere of influence and God's creation.

So, again in review:

⊙   *Malak*—To occupy our time with a skill or occupation

⊙   *Abad*—To till the ground. To tend in our profession.

⊙   *Shamar*—To keep watch or guard and protect.

We can see that God fully intended to work through humankind and the occupations that He entrusted to him. Genesis 2 is almost entirely devoted to the occupations of work. From the beginning, God had big plans for our occupations of work. We who are in Christ are destined to fulfill the call placed upon our lives on earth by finishing the work God created for us to do.

Job Descriptions

Originally, when God gave Adam and Eve their job description to fill the earth, subdue it and rule over it, He granted them dominion over the entire earth! What this means is God gave Adam and Eve sovereign authority over a domain or realm (of the earth).

(Again, it is curious to note that two and a half chapters before the fall, God's focus dealt with *creation* and *work*.) After God blessed them and gave them their job description, He said it was "very good."

From Genesis 1:28 and Genesis 2:15-17, we can see man's job description given as five commandments:

⊙ **First Commandment:** Genesis 1:28—Be fruitful. Prosper and be blessed to do well.

⊙ **Second Commandment:** Genesis 1:28—Multiply. Procreate and fill the earth.

⊙ **Third Commandment:** Genesis 1:28—Subdue the earth. Bring the earth under man's control as an extension of God's Spirit in the world.

⊙ **Fourth Commandment:** Genesis 2:15—Tend (*abad*) and keep (*shammar*) the garden. God placed man in the garden as a beach-head to guard and protect. Do not give up dominion to another. (God had an enemy in his garden: Satan.)

⊙ **Fifth Commandment:** Genesis 2:17—Do not eat of the Tree of the Knowledge of Good and Evil. This was a call to obedience, a test that Adam would fail.

Adam and Eve were given dominion over the garden, all the trees, all the plants, all the birds and all the animals. God had given Adam and Eve an incredible gift and an equally incredible responsibility.

This same responsibility before God is ours today. It is still God's desire that we would be fruitful and multiply by having children and filling the earth. We are still called to bring the earth under the control of God—as extensions of His spiritual dominion and authority. We are given that authority through Christ Jesus. We are also called to occupy (*malak*) tend and cultivate (*abad*) and guard and protect (*shammar*) God's original plan for the earth. We are called to obey these commands through the power of Jesus Christ in us.

God Shared His Sovereignty

The relationship between God, work and man is seen clearly in Genesis 2:19. Genesis 2:19 reads, *"Now the Lord God had formed out of the ground all the beasts of the field and the birds of the air. He brought them to the man to see what he would name them; and whatever the man called each living creature, that was its name."* God was sharing His sovereignty with Adam. In the Hebrew culture, there is no greater authority than to name an individual—even to this day.

In Daniel 1:7, we read how Daniel and his friends, after being captured, were immediately renamed. The Babylonian rulers understood the power they had over their captives even to the point of changing their names in an effort to try to change who they were. The power of Jesus' name is the supreme example. He instructed the disciples to pray in the name of Jesus Christ. It is in His name (in accordance with His will) that we are granted all power and authority.

God's original plan for humankind was to establish dominion through these concepts of work. God's desire was for man to fill the earth (His creation) with people who would, in turn, subdue the earth and rule over it. What happened to God's original intent and purposes? Did it change with the fall? How does the fall affect work? Did work change after the fall?

Not a Result of the Fall

There are several misconceptions regarding God's purposes for "work." One of these misconceptions is the notion that work was a result of the fall. Genesis 2:5 reveals that work was not a result of the fall, because in this passage God clearly intended humankind to work the ground even before He created them.

Work is not evil and should not be burdensome in our lives. God created work as something to occupy our time—thus the word "occupation." We were created to be in relationship with God but also to glorify God through our occupations. He created us with the intention that we would work. The very concept of work is a biblical one.

The idea that work was a result of the fall seems to leave many businesspeople with a mistaken impression that work was cursed and that working hard and producing wealth is worldly or ungodly. Some Christian businesspeople today feel they are looked upon as guilty of some sort of wrongdoing for being in a position of financial success.

Because Christian businesspeople work alongside

unbelievers and others in a society who may have built success through greed or manipulation, it is assumed that they also must have behaved in the same way to get ahead. Some have assumed that all successful businesspeople are corrupt. I have personally been asked the question, "How can you be ethical and still be successful in business?"

Not only is it possible to maintain a Christian witness and still produce wealth in business, it is imperative that we distinguish ourselves from unbelievers by our Christian witness in society through our ethics in work. Our culture is suffering from a lack of witness in every part of society. If we are to be a light to our nation, we must shine as an example of purity and excellence in all that we do.

Man Rebels

Why did humans rebel against God? Humans have always rebelled against God's established authority or rule, which He established through His works in the world. However, God in His grace and mercy wants us to reclaim his authority and rule and re-establish his "work" in the world.

Originally, in the garden, God offered Adam and Eve dominion and authority. With that offer came an ability to choose. God commanded them to eat of the fruit of the

Tree of Life, but instead, they chose the forbidden Tree of the Knowledge of Good and Evil.

Genesis 2:16 says, "And the Lord God **commanded the man**, saying, 'Of every tree of the garden you may freely eat.'" This included the Tree of Life, which is also the tree spoken of in Revelation 22.

Work was not cursed at the fall

Adam and Eve opted to eat from the Tree of the Knowledge of Good and Evil, which the Lord forbade. The result of that choice was spiritual death, just as God warned. The separation between God and man could not be repaired by human means.

In Genesis 3, we see one of the results of the fall. The result was a curse upon the earth. "Cursed is the ground for your sake, in toil you shall eat of it all the days of your life" (Gen. 3:17).

Having established earlier that work is indeed not a result of the fall, we must also take note, through this Scripture, that work was not cursed at the fall. It was the earth (or the ground) that was cursed. What did this mean for humanity? It meant the ground would no longer produce the way it once had. Now, man would have to work harder in order for the ground to produce. The ground changed, but God's original concept of work did not change. The fact is "work" is one of the very reasons we were created.

Major Changes

God's original stated purpose for humans to work did not change with the fall. However, the effort of work would change dramatically when humans lost their authority (dominion) in the fall. Man would now have to wait for the Messiah before he would once again be given authority on the earth.

Sadly, at this point in Scripture, we see the concept of work is no longer an occupation of man, (*malak*) but has become a **preoccupation** of man, even replacing fellowship with God. There was no room in Adam and Eve's life for preoccupation before the fall, because everything was in perfect balance. Now, because of the fall, man has to strive to bring balance to his life. Preoccupation turns us from fellowship with God and causes us to focus upon ourselves. It can tip our lives out of balance.

Adam knew the life altering isolation of being separated from God. Humanity was now left to fend for themselves because of sin.

Therefore the Lord God sent him out of the Garden of Eden to till (abad) *the ground from which he was taken. (Genesis 3:23)*

After the fall, we can see that humankind is still charged with the instruction to work (*abad*) the ground outside the garden. However, they had lost their job description to guard and protect (*shammar*) it.

In Genesis 4:24, God gave the job of guarding and protecting the garden to an angel. *"So He drove out the man; and He placed cherubim at the east of the Garden of Eden, and a flaming sword which turned every way, to guard the way to the tree of life."*

Man's Struggle

Why does work/occupation become so important after the fall? The answer is ***provision***. Man must now provide for himself for his very survival, because the earth and its productivity were cursed. God used to take care of all man's needs in the garden, but man forfeited this provision when he lost fellowship with God.

Satan, many times, takes advantage of this vulnerability, gaining entry into our lives by consuming us with survival needs. He suggests to us that our identity lies with our career or in what we can accomplish, rather than who we are in Christ. If we fall for this lie, our preoccupation can essentially push God out, and even become a replacement for God in our lives.

After the fall, humankind looked differently upon his work. In Genesis 4, man is described not just by his name, but also by his occupation. His very identity is now attached to his work. This impact was so strong that the first generation after the fall was identified this way.

Then she bore again, this time his brother Abel. Now Abel was a keeper of sheep, but Cain was a tiller of the ground. (Genesis 4:2)

Humankind had become preoccupied with work because their very existence depended upon it. This continues to be one of man's ongoing struggles in this life. Prior to the fall, Adam and Eve spent time with the Father in perfect fellowship. Work was not their preoccupation. Today, we must make a conscious effort to spend time in fellowship with God. Without daily interaction with God, we run the risk of becoming preoccupied with life, thereby losing our balance and perspective.

Work was never intended to be an opportunity to become self-serving, but rather an opportunity to serve God. If we keep our eyes focused on Jesus, we will maintain our balance in life.

Whatever your work, career, temporary job, volunteer job or whatever it is you do, do it in a way that will bring honor to God. Biblical principles were designed for us to follow in every part of our lives.

No matter what we do, there is always an opportunity to respectfully represent God's ways in daily living.

Our work and everything we do on this earth, we should do to glorify God.

[23]Whatever you do, work at it with all your heart, as working for the Lord, not for men, [24]since you know that you will receive an inheritance from the Lord as a reward. It is the Lord Christ you are serving. (Col. 3:23-24)

Finally, we see in Genesis 5:29 the continuation of how the concept of work continued to be a burden of survival. This mention of work is *abad*—tilling the ground or cultivating. We do not see here the (*shammar*) guarding and protecting.

In addition, he called his name Noah, saying, *"This*

one will comfort us concerning our work and the toil of our hands, because of the ground which the Lord cursed." (Gen. 5:29)

Humankind was reduced to a toilsome burden of work (*abad*) without the responsibility of guarding work (*shammar*). They needed comfort—They needed a redeemer.

Work Redeemed

Listen to the words of Jesus in John 5:17: "But Jesus answered them, 'My Father has been working until now, and I have been working.'" As stated earlier, God is the author and creator of work. It was never the *working* or the *prospering* that caused God heartache, but rather it was the rejection by man of God's ways for his own ways. Rebellion and selfish ambition break the heart of God. Jesus was our perfect example of obedience and He did the works of the Father.

Today, God has posted men and women in positions of responsibility and authority to complete work-work which He has ultimately begun.

Jesus was also called to finish the work that his Father had begun. In John 4:34, Jesus said to the disciples, *"My food is to do the will of him who sent me and to finish his work."* The distinction Jesus makes in this Scripture is between the fulfillment of physical food (which the disciples thought was his greatest need at that time) and the fulfillment Jesus received in fulfilling God's will, not His own. God's destiny for Jesus was fulfilled when Jesus finished His work.

We too, can only find true fulfillment in the work that God has preordained us to do on this earth. In John 5:19-20, Jesus also spoke of completing His Father's work.

Most assuredly, I say to you, the Son can do nothing of Himself, but what He sees the Father do; for whatever He does, the Son also does in like manner. For the Father loves the Son, and shows Him all things that He himself does; and He will show Him greater works than these, that you may marvel." (John 5:19-20)

The Father intended to fulfill His work through His Son, Jesus and Jesus obediently fulfilled it. Later, Jesus gave the same mandate to His followers.

"Most assuredly, I say to you, he who believes in Me, the works that I do he will do also; and greater works than these he will do, because I go to My Father." (John 14:12)

We now have the same mandate that Jesus had from the Father—to complete the work that He has begun. Going back to Genesis, God created the world and created man to work and manage the world—to do the work that He has set forth for us to do. We know this is possible today, because God has given us the gift of grace so that we can fulfill it. *"He who began a good work in you will be faithful to complete it" (Philippians 1:6).*

Today, God has posted men and women in positions of responsibility and authority to complete work—work which He has ultimately begun. Farmers are carrying on the work of tilling the soil. Physicians are carrying on God's work—even God performed surgery on Adam. Positions of government—No authority exists that was not established by God. Law enforcement—God is the ultimate lawgiver. And the list goes on.

Work and Rest

The very first concept of work is demonstrated in

Genesis 1:1 when God created the world. The act of creation is described (by God) as work. In Genesis 2:2-3, God rested from His work. Why did God rest? Was He tired?

God rested from all His work, which He had done, and He blessed the seventh day and sanctified it, because in it He rested from all His work, which God had created and made. (Gen. 2:2-3)

The idea that God was so pleased and called the work "very good" and blessed and sanctified the seventh day indicates that God was resting in the goodness and beauty of what He had done. As stated in Genesis 1:31, *"Then God saw everything that He had made, and indeed it was very good. So the evening and the morning were the sixth day."*

God saw all the beauty of the creation (the work of His hands). He saw the magnificent wonder of His work and ***He rested in it.***

God was not tired—He was marveling over His work. Adam and Eve understood this principle. They worked during the day and walked with God in the cool of the evenings. Their lives were in simple and perfect harmony. In addition, every need was taken care of by their

Father. Adam and Eve were experiencing the fulfillment of purpose and rest in their Father's will. They understood it because of the perfect example they had from their Father what it was to work and to rest.

To Retire or Not to Retire

What about our lives today? Is God calling us to rest in our work as well? Absolutely.

For many people, the idea of resting is an early retirement. Now, I am going to say something radical in a culture of people who spend their entire lives looking forward to the goal of a happy and hopefully early retirement: I believe the concept of retirement is a ploy of the enemy to keep us from the full purpose of God in our lives.

Nowhere in Scripture does God speak of retirement. Right up to the end of His life, Jesus said He and the Father were working. Nowhere in Old or New Testament examples do we see men and women of God retiring and heading off to the beach to sit and sip lemonade until they die. This concept of saving up enough resources to retire is a worldly one. Perhaps the type of work we do will change as we grow older, based upon our physical capabilities, but God is always at work in us, and we ought to always be at work for Him.

If we will walk in this principle of work and rest, we will be fulfilled and have no desire or need to retire. In fact, statistics show that men and women who quit work often die very much earlier than those who remain active and occupied.

The *rest* that God intends for us is also mentioned in Hebrews 4. The Lord has ordained a place of rest for His people to enter.

...although the works were finished from the foundation of the world. For He has spoken in a certain place of the seventh day in this way: "And God rested on the seventh day from all His works" and again in this place, "They shall not enter my rest." (Heb. 4:3-5)

Here we see the contrast between God's ordained plan for rest and the hardened hearts of humankind and the tendency to strive and not enter into it. The context of this Scripture in Hebrews is a warning and a correction to those who refuse to enter the rest, but instead, are perishing in their striving.

God's original design, from the beginning of time was that we would walk in His ways and rest in His will, just as He did. His design for work was one of beauty, creativity, fulfillment, and yes—rest.

Therefore, we can work without shame, be successful without greed and be a part of the big picture of God. We are his ambassadors in the workplace. So whistle while you work, rest in Christ and enjoy the blessing God has designed for you.

IX

Becoming God's Friend

s I travel the country, God has me regularly share a word of encouragement and challenge to congregations. I have seen at times more than 80 percent of a church respond to receive their calling and releasing for what God has designed them for as kings and queens.

As kings and queens, you are a vital force to be released on the earth to bring forth the kingdom of God. I believe today that the Lord is looking for friends on the earth. Like the patriarch Abraham who was a king, God desires our friendship to accomplish His will and to enjoy us as His sons and daughters.

¹³Greater love has no one than this, that he lay down his life for his friends. ¹⁴You are my friends if you do what I command. ¹⁵I no longer call you servants, because a servant does not know his master's business. Instead, I have called you friends, for everything that I have learned from my father I have made known to you. ¹⁶You did not choose me, but I chose you and appointed you to go and bear fruit that will last. Then the Father will give you whatever you ask in my name. ¹⁷This is my command: Love each other." (John 15:13-17)

This is the beginning of our discussion to show us the heart of the Father. He calls us His friends. God desires us to be His people who know His business. According to this text in the Bible, at least a portion of this business is to love each other. The loving of each other is the fruit that lasts.

As kings and queens, you are a vital force to be released on the earth to bring forth the kingdom of God.

God desires this intimacy with Him. So how do we get there? To answer this question we are going to have to

travel an entire day and night with our Lord and Savior
Jesus Christ.

The aforementioned day may seem long at times,
but the richness of its lessons to our lives as kings and
queens can be awesome! The day to which I am referring
is recorded in Matthew 14. It starts with the story of John
the Baptist being beheaded by Herod. In verse 12 we
read, *"John's disciples came and took his body and
buried it, then they went to tell Jesus."*

Before we go any further, let us talk about John and
Jesus' relationship. Remember John was family to Jesus,
cousins to be exact. Remember when Elizabeth saw Mary,
the mother of Jesus, and the child in her womb jumped at
the sound of Mary's voice? This must have been a family
discussion for many years in order for the writer to be able
to record it. They were both miracle children in the same
family.

John and Jesus grew up together. It is easy to
imagine some meals together. Playing in the backyard while
parents talked over meals. They knew each other well. I
am sure Jesus was proud of John as he preached and
became famous.

Remember that special day when Jesus started his
ministry? Jesus went to John to be baptized. These two
men were not only family, they were friends. What a great

scene where Jesus is baptized, and John sees a dove descend and hears God speak that this is His Son! I am sure the incident confirmed to John all the thirty years of family suspicion and stories about Jesus. Remember John is the one who stated, *"Behold the Lamb who takes away the sins of the world" (John 1:29).*

John knew who Jesus really was. At this point John's ministry decreased and Jesus' increased. Nevertheless, John continued to affirm Jesus, both publicly and privately. It was this friend, who probably could most relate to Jesus, who died.

As sudden, cruel and unjustifiable John's death was, I am sure the news of it riveted through Jesus' soul. Someone he genuinely loved and with whom He had close, fond and most likely fun memories of was now dead. Now let us continue with the rest of Jesus' day.

In verse 13, we see Jesus' immediate response. *"When Jesus heard what happened, he withdrew by boat privately to a solitary place."* I believe Jesus wanted to be alone, feel the pain, praying and process the news he just received. I think all of us in human terms can understand. In Jesus' view, John was the greatest among men. John definitely held a place in Jesus' heart that was now hurting from the loss. However, Jesus would not find solitude immediately.

In the rest of verse 13-14 we read, *"Hearing of this, the crowds followed him on foot from the towns. When Jesus landed and saw a large crowd, He had compassion on them and healed their sick."* Jesus was having what I call an interruption of His needs. These people were in need of healing and having their lives changed. Therefore, Jesus extended compassion and ministered to them, possibly for hours.

Now just stop minute, think of all the emotions that must have been exploding among the crowd as Jesus made the lame walk, and healed those sick from birth. The crowd may have gone wild with applause and rejoicing. What about a blind man who may have seen his first face that day, or a mother who hugged Jesus so tightly for healing her child? This would have given an incredible high to any minister anytime in history.

Then evening comes and the disciples tell Jesus to send away the crowds. However, Jesus, who has still not had private time to mourn the loss of his dear friend, decides to feed multitudes with five loaves and two fishes. Matthew 14:15-21 covers the close of this day in the life of Jesus:

[15]*As evening approached, the disciples came to him and said, "This is a remote place, and it's already getting*

late. Send the crowds away, so they can go to the villages and buy themselves some food."

[16]Jesus replied, "They do not need to go away. You give them something to eat." [17]"We have here only five loaves of bread and two fish," they answered. [18]"Bring them here to me," he said. [19]And he directed the people to sit down on the grass. Taking the five loaves and the two fish and looking up to heaven, he gave thanks and broke the loaves. Then he gave them to the disciples, and the disciples gave them to the people. [20]They all ate and were satisfied, and the disciples picked up twelve basketfuls of broken pieces that were left over. [21]The number of those who ate was about five thousand men, besides women and children.

Now how do you think that felt? We had a revival of miracles most of the day. The rest of the evening, Jesus partook of His miracle of eating fish and bread with the five thousand and the twelve disciples. Wow! What an earmark of a day for Jesus! However, the loss of His friend John was still with Him. Verses 22 and 23 continue, *"Immediately Jesus made the disciples get into the boat and go ahead of him to the other side, while He dismissed the crowd. After He had dismissed them he went up on the mountainside by himself to pray."*

I can only imagine the prayer of Jesus that evening. I am sure He thanked the Father for the tremendous day of ministry; for the men, women and children who were healed and set free from whatever ailed them that day. I am sure he praised the Father for the miracle of feeding the five thousand. I am also sure He talked to his Father about John. I can hear him saying, "Father I loved John. He was my friend. He was the only man on earth who truly knew who I am. I feel so alone now," and on and on as He grieved and shared his pain with the Father.

In verse 24 we get to look back at what is going on with the disciples: *"...but the boat was already a considerable distance from land, buffeted by the waves because the wind was against it."*

As kings and queens, I am sure many of us can relate to being placed in a situation (boat) by Jesus and feeling as if the storms of life are against us. Often it seems in hindsight that God was just about ready to give you a new revelation regarding who He is. That is what happened to our unsuspecting disciples as the waves pressed against them.

"During the fourth watch of the night Jesus went out to them, walking on the lake" (verse 25).

Jesus was up praying and now goes to rejoin his brave disciples at about 3:00 A.M. What is interesting to note is the disciples' reaction to Jesus walking on water.

"When the disciples saw him walking on the lake, they were terrified. 'It's a ghost," they said, and cried out in fear" (Matt.14:26). Wow! What a reaction. This was a bad night getting worse. I mean their confusion had to be excruciating. After all, they have never seen anyone walk on water before. The Jesus they knew was about to break all the rules of gravity and life itself.

I can tell you that as kings and queens your paradigms will often be challenged and changed when you follow Jesus. Sometimes it feels like He puts you in a corner and then walaa! He brings you into a new understanding of his God-ship. Now these people were not just saying, "Hey look at the ghost—hmmm, interesting." They were screaming their lungs out, thinking they were going to die. Can you imagine Matthew stammering, "It's, it's, it's, a gh...gho...ghost!"

Peter has faith to believe that miracles were not just for Jesus.

Then Jesus spoke some reality into the situation in verse 27. *"Take courage! It is I. Don't be afraid."*

Now let me tell you the spirit in which this was done, the way I see it. I see Jesus just coming from a great prayer time. He probably even lifted each one of these men up in prayer just minutes or an hour ago. He is having a great time exercising some of His God-ship by walking on the water. I do not think Jesus had a religious or shaming heart when He reassured them who He was. I think He would have had a great grin on His face saying, "C'mon guys, it's Me! Relax!"

Then the story turns to another character who is going to teach us how to become a friend of God, not just a follower of Christ. Peter, that all-heart-after-God kind of person, steps into the pages of spiritual history again. Peter's response to Jesus' reassuring voice was "Lord, if it's you tell me to come to you on the water."

There is so much here to be said about these few comments. These simple words transformed Peter and Jesus' relationship forever. Let us first look at what Peter actually said. He did not call Jesus rabbi or teacher, but Lord. Peter was beginning to understand, much like John the Baptist, who this Jesus was. He was really the only one worthy of worship. Peter knew Jesus was the Lord, Lord of all the earth and Lord of Peter himself.

I think it is interesting that Peter asked the Lord to tell him to come on the water with him. Peter may be impetuous but he is not foolish. He knew if he was obeying Jesus then the supernatural could happen. He knew by now the power of Jesus' word. He has seen sickness submit to His word, demons submit to His word, even five loaves submit to His word just hours ago. He knew the word of the Lord was life, truth and trustworthy.

What I also find amazing is that Peter has faith to believe that miracles were not just for Jesus. He believed that miracles could be for himself as well. After all, Jesus had done miracles in Peter's business with the fish jumping into his net. By now, this disciple may have seen healing and deliverance occur through his own voice and hands as he obeyed Jesus day in day out.

Therefore, Peter could now believe that "If Jesus can do it, and I am obeying Him, I can do it as well." Would to God all the kings and queens of the earth from every nation have this faith in their lives, families, business and ministry. Would to God the kings and queens prayed for the sick and they be well. This is the day of revival that I am looking forward to in the ministry of kings and queens everywhere. When the power and miraculous flow through the kings and queens of the earth, whether they are em-ployee or employer and have faith to believe that they are the agents for the greatest revival in history, then the revival of kings and queens can happen!

I get so excited about this! Let us go back to the story and look at not only what was said, but also who was saying it, and some of the very dynamics these words had on these two men. Remember, Peter was a fisherman. He grew up on the water. He probably had been fishing since he was a young man and had witnessed plenty of times of rough, unrelenting waves and storms. He may have even seen boats wash onto the shore without the men in it.

Peter knew that to step out on this water in the natural could be certain death. He knew unless Jesus was really God, he could die. This was Peter saying to Jesus, "If it's you Lord, God Almighty, I will risk my whole life, everything I think is real and true for you!" This was not just stepping out of the boat; this was possibly ending his life. Notice Peter was the only one who could make the paradigm shift that Jesus was God. If in obeying Him anything is possible, even risking your life is safe if He commands such of you.

I must say Peter seems to have been the bravest, most passionate and really the most advanced of all the disciples in the supernatural. He knew who Jesus really was. Therefore, with all this happening, Jesus has a response: *"Come" (verse 29)*.

The verse continues, *"Then Peter got down out of the boat, walked on the water and came toward*

Jesus." Wow! What a miracle! There have only been two men in history to walk on water and Peter was one of them. Peter was the only one willing to participate in the miracle, while the other eleven were only willing to witness a miracle. Now Peter's faith may not have been perfect, but it was definitely much stronger than that of the others. He was willing to risk it all to obey Jesus' command.

The story goes on in verse 30: *"But when he saw the wind, he was afraid and, beginning to sink, cried out, 'Lord save me!"* I truly do not think anyone would have done much better in these circumstances. I remember sharing this sermon once and a brother in the Lord came up and reminded me, "It says he *began* to sink, not that he *sank."* I do not know about you, but I probably would have instantly sunk. I think this was an interesting point.

What is also interesting is that Peter, again from the depths of his heart, establishes who Jesus is, Lord. Instead of screaming out, "I'm going to die!" Peter's reaction to the life-threatening situation is "Lord."

When you are in the midst of a life-or-death situation, whatever is in your heart will come out. What came out of Peter's heart once again was his belief in Jesus' lordship.

"Immediately" with not even a flash of thought, Jesus was there to help His friend Peter. Verse 31 says,

"Immediately Jesus reached out his hand and caught him. 'You of little faith,' he said, 'why did you doubt?'" Now the latter sentence needs to be interpreted in context.

Here is Jesus after a great prayer time seeing one of His disciples really grasp the concept of His identity, and like a proud friend or father, I do not think Jesus' tone was critical, pompous or religious. So often, I hear this verse preached with such a tone. I believe just the opposite. I think that Jesus, with a big grin and smile, was saying to Peter, "Why did you waver? We were just getting started." You know what I mean, the kind of statement a dad might make when teaching his son to throw a ball, "Hey why did you let the ball go in the lake? You were just getting the hang of it. Come here. I love you, son, you knucklehead." I truly don't feel this was a rebuke but rather a term of affection between friends.

The story continues in verse 32: *"And when they climbed into the boat, the wind died down. Then those in the boat worshiped him saying, 'Truly you are the Son of God.'"* This is great. The spectators are finally getting it too. They worshiped Jesus. I want to look at why. Was it because Jesus walked on water? Or healed the sick that day? Or was it the feeding of the five thousand just hours ago? Or because the winds stopped when they entered the boat? All of these answers may be part of it.

At this point, most of the disciples had figured out that Jesus is different, and He does different things. They would probably believe Jesus could walk on water.

I think there was another crucial element, and that was Peter himself. They knew Peter and they knew that he could in no way walk on water. They knew for that to happen, God must be behind it. Peter walking on water was a great miracle.

It amazes me here that it took one person to break out of his comfort zone so others could worship Jesus. I think this is so appropriate.

It takes one person, man or woman to believe God. They need to step out of their comfortable uninvolved boat to allow others to worship. It is the man who teaches people to read English by using the Bible, the woman who goes to the women's prison cell, the woman who starts a small group to teach young mothers some basic life skills. It is the man who uses his previous addiction to reach out to those still trapped that allows people to come to Christ and worship Him.

What if Peter would have stayed in his boat? What if he, like the others that day, only wanted to watch the miracles? Then eleven people would have had less of a revelation of who God is.

How many kings and queens have forfeited their

ministry and kept others from not seeing Jesus? See, you are the kings and queens of your city, state and nation. It is TOTALLY up to you. If you don't get out of the boat, who will? You are the closest to the lost, broken and needy in your community. You are the solution for a small group, whether it is a home Bible study, Sunday school class, teaching young men how to start a business, or any of the hundreds of ideas your church or community needs. You are kings and queens; you see the needs, and often what you see spiritually, you are responsible for spiritually. Therefore, I encourage you to get out of the boat and jump in.

Be the only sea-stained, wet, trying, worshiper of God from your boat. Do not look at what others in the boat are doing. They are spectators. As a king or queen, you have a ministry, and sitting in the pew is not it. I see nowhere that kings and queens are to just give money, warm a pew and watch the priests. You are to be about your God-given mandate. Start implementing your ideas! Dare to make your dream a reality! Go for it! Get wet!

As a king or queen, you have a ministry, and sitting in the pew is not it.

Now I want to shift gears to go back to the beginning of Jesus' day when John the Baptist's disciples informed Him that His friend had died. Jesus tried to find some solitude, but being interrupted by the crowds, He healed them, fed them and then dismissed them. He went to pray and pour out His grief to God. Then Peter steps out of the boat and straight into the heart of Jesus. Peter became the replacement of John, the friend who knew Jesus intimately. Who had the revelation that Jesus was the Son of God? Peter did. To whom did Jesus say, "Upon this rock I will build my church?" It was Peter. Peter knew that his friend's heart and business was to love others.

If you don't get out of the boat, who will?

Let us go back to where we started in John 15:13-17. I think now we know it takes getting out of the boat to be the friend of God, and that we need to get rid of our paradigms, history and ideas, and trust the word of the Lord and His calling of us into the waters of ministry. Let us review these verses:

13Greater love has no one than this, that he lay down his life for his friends. 14You are my friends if you do what I command. 15I no longer call you servants, *because a servant does not know his master's business. Instead, I have called you friends, for everything that I learned from my Father I have made known to you. ¹⁶You did not choose me, but I chose you and appointed you to go and bear fruit—fruit that will last. Then the Father will give you whatever you ask in my name. ¹⁷This is my command: Love each other. (John 15:13-17)*

You see, when we lay down our lives by getting out of the boat and loving people we become the friends of God. According to this passage of Scripture, loving others is the family business of God. In other words, as children of our Father's business or industry, our job is to love them.

Some of us kings and queens are business owners. Is it not a great day when your kids want to become involved in the family business, not just for the pay, but because they really enjoy it? Hasn't Jesus through His death and resurrection clearly made known to us the business of loving others?

You are the kings and queens of the earth. Without your ministry your church, community and nation suffers. If we live only for ourselves and do not release Christ in us through some form of touching others, what kind of kings or queens would we be?

Ministry of Kings and Queens

I encourage you as a king to seek the heart of God for your usefulness in the family business of loving the world and church. Find your kingly or queenly ministry so the revival of God can come to you and through you. I really believe it is when we rise and take our place in ministry that our churches will grow through people being saved and touched.

I want to lead you in a prayer: "Jesus I ask you to release your kingly/queenly ministry through me. I want to get out of the boat. Please give me the eyes to see what you see and willingness to love people where you direct me. I am open to your will for me. Amen."

I pray God uses you all the days of your life. I love being in the family business of loving people. God will show you His will. He will guide you! Welcome to the kingly ministry!

X

When Kings & Queens Come to My Church
By Ted Haggard

 ery often, we pastors feel like the local churches we serve are our babies. We love the church, we want to see it grow, and we sometimes feel like very little care about the success of the church as much as we do. We have wonderful leadership teams and support staffs, and our volunteers are selfless and determined to fulfill God's calling. However, at the end of the day, that dreaded feeling surfaces that makes us fear that it is all up to us. *We* have to make the church work. *We* have to make it run well. We know in our heads that the church belongs to God, but we have spent so much

time, energy, emotion, and money to make everything just right that we must personally ensure that no one foolishly messes this up.

We are set up. We are trapped. The war is on. We feel the battle within ourselves between control and trust, restriction and freedom, needing to do it ourselves or allowing others to do the work.

On a Sunday morning a few years ago, I was upstairs in my office praying a few minutes before the worship service. My notes were prepared, the praise and worship team was ready to go, and the technical team was hovering around the soundboard making final arrangements. It was a normal Sunday morning, and everything was in place for a good service.

I was supposed to train them to be ministers themselves.

As I paced back and forth praying, I glanced outside and watched people parking their cars, getting out and walking into the building. Suddenly, God gave me a revelation. I was not supposed to merely go downstairs and pastor the people that morning. I was not supposed to just minister to them as I did every week. I was supposed to train them to be ministers themselves. I needed to pastor these people in order to fulfill my calling, but more importantly, I needed to help them find their own callings and learn the joy and excitement of pastoring the people around them. Why? Because I could never reach the people they could reach. I worked in church and para-church circles 90 percent of the time, but the members of my church lived their lives out in the workplaces, schools, and public places of our city. The only way to really get into the lives of the people in our city was to train our church members to minister in their immediate environment everyday.

That morning led to months and years of changes in the way ministry is structured at New Life Church. Most significantly, we changed our small group ministry into a free market system where any individual in our church can start a small group based on any topic and use it to disciple others. We knew that, for instance, while the unchurched people who play basketball at the YMCA may never attend our church, they would join a basketball club. In addition, if that club were led by a New Life Church member, that member could subtly share the gospel and affect fellow basketball enthusiasts people for Jesus. The same was true for everyone highly involved in the various arenas of our city, from the business and political community to the skateboarding community.

We now have over 900 of these small groups, and

the number increases every semester (our groups follow the semester format of our local schools so people can enter and exit easily every few months). The topics of those groups range from Bible studies and prayer groups to book clubs, mountain bike clubs, auto mechanic clubs and hospital ministry teams. If someone has a good idea, he or she can start a group after a quick afternoon-long training session and background check. Why is it so easy and open? Because God showed me that day in my office that I am not the exclusive source of ministry in our church, I do not just want to tell people how to serve God—I want to give them a place and a mechanism they can use to discover and sharpen their gifts and use them to expand the kingdom of God. I have no desire to control the calling and gifts of the people God sends to our congregation; I just want to empower them to grow in their calling so we can reach more people together than I ever could alone.

Our new limited control environment has revolution-ized the strength of ministry throughout our church. In addition, the open doors have ensured that new kings, queens, and priests flood in every year. That means not simply that our church numbers are growing, but that kings, queens, and priests are using New Life as their home base to do the work of God all over the world.

I love this concept of kings and priests that you

have been reading about in this book. Kings and queens focus most of their time and efforts outside the walls of the church, while priests focus the majority of their energies within the confines of more traditional ministry styles. The members of New Life know that our church is filled with kings, queens and priests, that both are equally valuable; thus it's my job to help all of them discover their roles and to help them do their ministries. It is a great, life-giving system.

Of course, it only works if we can actually help people discover their role. Particularly when kings and queens come through the door, it can be tricky to help them feel at home and to see how God wants to use their talents and interests to expand His kingdom. When kings and queens discover their gifts and feel that they are free to use those gifts, they go for it, and extraordinary things happen. But in order to see them go for it, we often have to retrain them from the clergy/laity mentality into the understanding that we all are ministers, we all have ministry roles, and we all need to work together in order to fulfill God's full plan. Obviously, in order to do this we have to overcome some of the usual pitfalls kings and queens face in churches—lack of acceptance, encouragement, and opportunity—and learn to relate to them in a way that liberates them to use their gifts to serve God.

Acceptance

All people want is to be accepted for who they are, not just for what they do. I do not love my son Marcus because he is an accomplished pianist; I love him because he is Marcus. People like Marcus—people who have outstanding gifts or blessings—can often feel like they have to perform in order to be loved. This can definitely be a problem with kings and queens, who may feel like they are loved for their money or public prestige. However, the kings and queens who attend New Life know that I love them for who they are: I love their heart for God, their desire to do ministry and their sensitivity to the Spirit of God in their lives. The kings and queens at New Life are people who I would be friends with anyway—I am just pleased that we get to be friends and do ministry together, too.

Now, this might sound a little goofy, but when I tell someone I love him or her, I *really* tell him or her. I un-abashedly, unashamedly proclaim my love and acceptance of them. I tell them how much I like them, how much I love their company, how excited I am to be living life with them. There is no doubt in their minds about how I feel—I am genuinely happy to have them in my life and in my church, and they know it.

Kings and queens need acceptance not based on

their accomplishments or giving records, but on who they are as people and as significant ministers in His Kingdom. Jesus accepted and loved unconditionally, and that is our model for ministry. When people know they are really accepted for who they are, they relax. They do not have to perform, and somehow that unleashes their desire to touch others and fulfill God's calling on their lives.

Encouragement

The difference between accepting someone and encouraging them is the same difference between being acquainted with someone and becoming their friend. In order to encourage someone, you have to find out about his or her world. What is it they really do? What are they interested in? Take the time to find out what gifts God has given the kings and queens in your church; then encourage them to be themselves. You will be surprised at the amazing talent and diversity existing within the kings and queens of the church, and you will be pleased at how much the church is strengthened when they are given opportunity to use their talents inside and outside the church.

In church culture, kings and queens are rarely encouraged for their success because many people assume they are just interested in increased profits. However, this is a cynical view, and it does not belong within church doors. Kings and queens are people who are legitimately serving God. Often God has very directly given them their business ideas so that they can bless and establish His kingdom in specific ways.

Kings and queens need to know that Christ did not just arbitrarily put them in the workplace. He put them there for a reason, and their calling is a high calling. When they understand their role in God's plan, their life will make spiritual sense like never before, and they will be unleashed to pursue the work of God in creative ways.

Opportunity

Kings and queens are doers. They are enterprising people. They are filled with creative ideas about serving God in a practical, life-giving fashion. I have had some of my most exciting ministry conversations with kings and queens. They are unconventional, industrious, intelligent and able ministers. Many of my closest friends are kingly because they constantly inspire me to do the work of God in new ways.

However, sometimes their potential is untapped. Sometimes their creative energies lay dormant inside them because no one has ever stimulated them outside of the business world. However, as their pastors, we have a great opportunity to remind them that God has a plan for their lives, and that the Christian life is about risk-taking and doing the impossible for God. We need to give kings and queens a chance to try out their gifts and encourage them in the process by opening the floodgates of opportunity.

I would much rather coach someone after a failed attempt than preclude the person from ever trying.

Of course, encouraging kings and queens to take risks means cleaning up after mistakes. It means doing some careful coaching when things do not turn out as planned. However, it is worth it. I would much rather coach someone after a failed attempt than preclude the person from ever trying.

Give kings and queens the opportunity to love the people they are called by God to serve. When kings and queens actively love skateboarders, homeschoolers, or whoever fits with their interests, amazing ministry happens. Help them see that it is okay to respond to that nagging dream within them. If they have always wanted to build a coffee shop to attract high schoolers in order to minister to them, encourage them to do it. If they want to take junior high boys camping in the mountains, coach them on discipleship and give them the opportunity they need. That is our job: to empower kings, queens, and priests alike to be about their ministry. Provide the opportunity, accept that it will be different, exciting, and unpredictable, and ride the wave.

Being a Friend, Being a Pastor

The bottom line is that when kings and queens come to my church I do not treat them any differently than I do anyone else. I try to be their pastor and I try to be their friend. I encourage them in reading the Bible and making God's Word the foundation of their lives. I encourage them to seek God through a lifestyle of prayer and fasting. I coach them on living a lifestyle of worship and commitment to the fulfillment of God's plan on the earth.

At the same time, I enjoy their company, joke with them and treat them with warmth and affection. I do not see them as different, but I do see them as outstanding and capable of doing extraordinary things for God. I try to open them up, stimulate them, giving them an opportunity to develop and exercise their strengths. I listen to their brainstorm of ideas for ministry and encourage them to actually use those ideas. I grant permission to experiment with new ministry ideas. In short, I rev them up and then let them take off for God, and our church is always better as a result.

XI

Responsibility of Royalty

 oyalty is truly what we are as kings and queens of the Most High God. We are His sons and daughters and He is our Father who happens to own the cattle on a thousand hills, the King of all kings throughout time and our God. He is royalty in the truest sense. He is above all, there is no question of His will on earth and He will ultimately assess all who ever lived.

Although most of us at this point might feel a hearty amen to whom He is, we sometimes feel unworthy of own royalty. He is our Father, and He is a king. I know that sounds simple, but that truly is the truth of the matter. We, through Christ, have the most royal blood flowing through our bodies; we are blood-purchased and blood royal. For if we accept His purchase we must accept our royalty through Him. Although this is true, I am amazed at how many Christians pull back and shy away from the truth of whose they are on the earth.

Try it sometime. Go up to another believer in Christ and welcome them in a kingly language, "King Bob, how are you doing today?" and watch Bob's reaction. Watch the awkwardness he feels. His response can be anything from "I'm no king" or "I don't know what you mean."

The kingly and queenly have so lost their royalty. They are almost embarrassed to be called what they are, kings and queens of the earth. I have seen this regardless of age, income or gender.

This seems peculiar to me. In the priestly, we have no problem with pastor, evangelist, prophet, bishop, father or other terms, distinguishing and giving honor to the priestly. They seem to accept their titles and roles in the body of Christ rather easily.

So what is the issue? I believe the issue is the kings and queens are not identified, nor do they feel secure with their identity. We as kings feel awkward, insecure and lacking confidence in our role as kings or queens. If we sat around and called each other King Bob, King Joe, Queen Mary, Queen Alice, we might begin to gain confidence and, more importantly, begin to take responsibility for our royalty.

This is what the next few pages are about, taking responsibility for who we are. I remember my wife and me attending the movie, *Princess Diaries.* It is about a teen-age girl who was being raised in America but was really a true princess of a European nation. Her mother and grandmother reveal the truth to her and let her decide whether to remain an average high school student, or to accept her identity and take her rightful place with the responsibilities of royalty. I feel the Lord wants each of us kings and queens to choose the latter, to realize who we are as His royalty on the earth. To assist you in this, we will examine several areas where royalty and responsibility go hand in hand for the kingly.

1. Knowing Whom You Are: Royalty

A king or queen for that matter must know who they are. This is critical for them to function as a royalty. They, inside themselves, must be secure that they have been given the gifts, talents, and responsibility to rule and serve in their sphere of influence.

A king or queen at first may feel unworthy, awk-ward in their role or insecure about their ability to rule. All

173

of us have seen movies or read books about real or fictitious kings who start off wobbly but somewhere along the way they get it. They get that they really are the king or queen of their kingdom, that they can reign and serve with confidence and that all they influence can be better because they accept their place.

Imagine if men and women in the body of Christ really understood their royalty. How might they view the significance of their life, their parenting, their friendships, their possessions, or money? If they were royalty they would think, and behave much differently. If you accepted your royalty, you might not allow certain areas of sin to exist in your life because it does not become royalty. It might not become royalty to do this or that or have this or that attitude so you do not do it because you accept your royalty. After all royalty cannot have traits of controlling, prejudice, unkindness, adultery or foolishness. That is just not acceptable for royalty. I know this sounds strange but as a king or queen who was made royal by the death of the King of Kings, and we accept our God-given royalty it changes us.

When we accept that we are kings and queens of God in this world, we become different. We process our choices differently. We behold the mundane with grace instead of contempt. Our vocations, homes and ministry outlets are now kingdom expressions and we are the

174

servant kings responsible for these.

After all royalty cannot have traits of controlling, prejudice, unkindness, adultery or foolishness. That is just not acceptable of royalty.

When we accept that we are who we are, it affects everything we do, including the very way we think. "Would a king do that? Would a royal queen behave in such a manner?" These are our questions on a daily basis, and they can quickly mold us to the nature and behavior of our God and King, Jesus Christ. We are His bloodline of royalty. When you get this it changes, truly changes the way you see yourself and quickly moves into your heart to be a better servant to everyone because you are of royal descent. It is becoming of royalty to be at their best for everyone they are given to influence.

2. Knowing Your Kingly Purpose

All of us who are kingly have a God-given purpose. Many of us are familiar with the motto "God has a plan for your life." Yet how many believe and behave with this in mind? How many Christians commonly called "laity" believe their job, business, gifting or parenting ability is significant to God?

See, when you accept royalty it gives everything a purpose. Where you are, and whom you touch right now is your royal purpose. You decide to accept or resist this. If you are flipping burgers or working a menial job right now, remember all kings go through training. It is in the training process that we often discover our purpose.

I remember going to Bible college and then seminary and really feeling God leading me to go to school. During this period of training for my kingship, God was exposing purpose. In both college and seminary, other men were always hanging out in my dorm room wanting advice, counsel, wisdom and discipleship. It was strange, but when God showed me this, it helped me piece together that my kingly calling had something to do with touching and healing hearts of men. This of course now is my kingly ministry through counseling, seminars and media. I did not know then that I was royalty, but God was faithful to expose His kingly purpose during my time of training.

Nevertheless, how do we find our kingly purpose? One way is to ask yourself two questions.

1.   What does the body of Christ ask from me regu larly? (Note: It is not "What do I want to do for the church?")

176

2.   What does the culture ask of you? What do friends, family, people at work ask from you regularly?

Does the church ask you to serve on committees, or to help set up chairs, or teach classes or drive the buses? Does your job always ask you to lead, manage and smooth things out or follow, support and encourage those around you? Take a minute and ask yourself this. This may be tied to your skills and give you a clue as to your kingly ministry.

Try to clearly separate your own desires from what people ask of you. Sometimes our desire to be something is very different from our true purpose. I remember a king with whom I went to seminary. He wanted to preach, teach or do anything pertaining to upfront ministry. Yet when he would do any of this, there was little to no life at all in it. On the other hand, he could fix just about anything. He had a side business of a handyman and construction company. What the church regularly asked of him was to drywall, run wires or paint. He paid his bills his whole life by the manual labor of constructing, building and repairing structures.

He did not like his kingly calling, but he was so anointed at it and had unquestionable authority when doing these jobs. God anointed his hands to fix almost anything, yet he rejected his kingly calling to pursue a priestly calling that never really created any life. I personally love every king who does electrical, drywall or woodworking because I consider them geniuses!

Whether you are in training or still early in your development find your purpose. When it is clear as to why God made you, often the anointing and authority develop in you for that task. It may consist of being a salesperson, real estate developer, public school teacher, nurse or secretary. I know people in all areas of life who are truly kings or queens in their areas of influence. My brother-in-law, David Schaffer, is a teacher in Pennsylvania. He has taught math for over two decades in the same school. He has been made a team leader of the math department, and is asked to serve in many areas in his school. He has unquestionable authority given to him when he is serving in his kingly calling and prays over the school every day as he walks the halls before anyone else arrives.

My other brother-in-law, Donald Brown, owns a home building company. He has never advertised and has God's supernatural anointing to build and construct homes and offices. Yet another brother-in-law, Lynn Kuster, is an anointed pharmacist in a hospital. He is consistently promoted and intuitively understands his industry and has been given by God favor in his industry. In addition, my sister-in-law Sandy Martinez is the most anointed administrative assistant to presidents of companies that you will ever meet.

I use these only to illustrate kingly calls. How about my father-in-law, Harold Schaffer, who was the best parts manager for car dealerships? He can still remember part numbers from years ago and was king of customer service. Everyone has a sphere of influence that God has given specifically to him or her.

I encourage you to find your kingly or queenly purpose. When you discover purpose, you often discover whom you are to serve. These are whom you are called to touch in a royal manner for our King.

3. Knowing Kingly Protocol

Being royalty does have the burden of protocol. After all, royalty must know what fork to use, how to address people, the procedures for stately business. The list goes on and on. These are definitely matters for earthly monarchs over current nations. For our royalty the kingly protocol goes much deeper. Unlike kings of this world, our God does not prioritize procedures as much as he prioritizes relationships with people.

Jesus, when asked about the most important issues in life, said, "Love God with all your heart" and "Love your neighbor as yourself" (Matt. 22:37-39).

Ministry of Kings and Queens

Love is of the greatest importance for kings and queens. Our heavenly Father has little value for forks, spoons and such, but tremendous concern about how we follow the greatest of protocol in the kingdom of God, love.

This love protocol goes in two directions. The first is to love God. A king or queen who does not spend time worshiping and loving God regularly is not following royal protocol. Royalty must seek and chase after God in order to worship and spend time with our King. I desire this daily. I love to love God, to tell him so, sit before Him and learn from Him. Fulfilling this first directive makes it more possible to carry out protocol number two, loving your neighbor.

Who is my neighbor? I think Jesus clears up this issue in the story of the Good Samaritan. All members of humanity, regardless of race, gender, social status or religion, are our neighbors. Royal protocol therefore is to love all people.

After all God is love. He is our King and He loves everyone. He models for us sacrifice and the loving of others. So how does a king or queen know if they are following protocol number two? I think Paul, in 1 Corinthians 13, gives us great insight to evaluate our progress.

[1]If I speak in the tongues of men and of angels, but have not love, I am only a resounding gong or a clanging cymbal. [2]If I have the gift of prophecy and can fathom all mysteries and all knowledge, and if I have a faith that can move mountains, but have not love, I am nothing. [3]If I give all I possess to the poor and surrender my body to the flames, but have not love, I gain nothing.

[4]Love is patient, love is kind. It does not envy, it does not boast, it is not proud. [5]It is not rude, it is not self-seeking, it is not easily angered, it keeps no record of wrongs. [6]Love does not delight in evil but rejoices with the truth. [7]It always protects, always trusts, always hopes, always perseveres. [8]Love never fails. But where there are prophecies, they will cease; where there are tongues, they will be stilled; where there is knowledge, it will pass away.

[9]For we know in part and we prophesy in part, [10]but when perfection comes, the imperfect disappears. [11]When I was a child, I talked like a child, I thought like a child, I reasoned like a child. When I became a man, I put childish ways behind me. [12]Now we see but a poor reflection as in a mirror; then we shall see face to face.

181

Now I know in part; then I shall know fully, even as I am fully known. [13]*And now these three remain: faith, hope and love. But the greatest of these is love.*

Being kingly does have its responsibilities. The protocol of love is the protocol of royalty. We get to serve God with love and worship and serve all others with love and respect. Royalty is obligated to follow protocol even when he or she feels differently. Therefore, to love is above what we think about another. This protocol may feel burdensome but when practiced will release your kingly ministry in everyone. It becomes a blessing for others to connect to you.

4. Accepting Responsibility

Accepting responsibility is often the hardest thing for the kingly. Accepting their gifting, their calling, their anointing and their importance in history is difficult. Too often only the priestly have owned the Bible stories of Joseph, Moses, David and Jesus. We have looked through the eyes of the priestly and have not seen ourselves.

We are the kingly, and the Bible definitely highlights our value and importance of not only being a part of the kingdom of God but also in helping to further the kingdom:

182

the salespeople, office managers, blue-collar workers, white-collar workers, employees and entrepreneurs. We are here not only to warm a pew and pay tithes, but also to do miracles, speak the truth and be an example of a powerful and godly life. Our stories are that which fill the pages of God's Word.

We're here not only to warm a pew and pay tithes, but also to do miracles, speak the truth, and be an example of a powerful and godly life.

What does this have to do with accepting responsibility you might ask? Everything! Until you see yourself as the royal of the Bible, being raised up to do the supernatural, you will have little faith for your life to be miraculous and significant to the kingdom of God.

You are the kitchen help who rebuilds your city (Nehemiah); you are the judge who fights off the enemies of your city (pornography, abortion, segregation); you are the business owner who hears God (12 disciples); you are the woman who encourages kings (2 Kings 22:14-20); you are the parents who can raise godly children (Joseph and Mary). You need to see that God is depending on you to accept your responsibilities.

183

I believe everyone reading this book is destined by God to utilize their sphere of influence for aggressively loving their culture. That may include having a family, church, city, state, national, or worldwide impact!

I really believe this because this is my experience with God. I remember I had just started a counseling practice that helped men get free from addiction, and the Lord told me to start praying for that city, and they came. Then I was told to pray for the state and the nation, and men with addictions flew from all over the country, seeking my professional assistance. Last year I was told by the Lord to pray for the nations, and now I travel regularly to conduct conferences on the topics of my books, *Intimacy* and *Sex, Men & God.*

What was happening to me was that I was incrementally taking responsibility for this area of touching lives. I fully accept that I am responsible to "heal the land," which is my mandate from the Living God. The type of healing has expanded significantly, as well as what God meant by "the land."

I tell you this to help motivate you. Maybe you feel your sphere of influence is small right now. Accept it as your current mandate, pray over all you do and pray for others who do the same thing. If you are a parts manager, pray for all the parts managers in your city. If you are a lawyer, pray for all the lawyers. You know better than anyone does what his or her needs are. Send them cards; make calls to these other people within your vocation. You would be amazed at your royal ministry if that were all you did.

I want to encourage you to take a minute and think, "What are my spheres of influence right now? How can I pray for those in my sphere of influence? How can God use me to love them and improve their lives?" Write down your thoughts. Make some goals. Then call a friend or mentor and have them hold you accountable to taking action in these areas for 100 days.

1. I am kingly/queenly.
2. The people I am kingly/queenly with are?
3. I can practically love them by:
4. I will pray for these at _____ (time each day)

I know this may seem strange at first, but try it. Believe you are royalty, and believe you are responsible. When you believe and accept responsibility, your life will change and the lives of others will be improved. Remember John 15:13: "Greater love has no one than this, that he lay down his life for his friends."

5. Kingly View

Kings or queens can see down generational lines. They have a strong sense of family as being important...not just their own children but also their grandchildren and great, great grandchildren, whom they may never see.

Family is important in the natural royal succession because "as the king so the country." Kings and queens know if their heirs are undisciplined, irresponsible or ungodly that the kingdom will suffer, and many lives depend on them. Many of us have watched the movie, *Prince of Egypt*. There was a scene where Pharaoh, Moses' legal father, was dealing with the older son who would be the next Pharaoh, and he says something to the effect, "It only takes one weak link to bring down a dynasty."

This Pharaoh knew that to be a king was to make sure that your heirs could rule successfully. This would take intention, commitment, time, education and resources. The sacrifices were worth it to have the peace that your kingdom would grow and prosper under your heirs.

This is an important part of being kingly and queenly. If everything you do has generational focus, your daily choices will be impacted for the better. How many monarchs wouldn't cheat on their spouse or file for divorce because of what it would do to the kingdom? Our marriage behavior is also important. Look at Vashti's consequence when she did not honor her position, and Ahab's relinquishing himself in his marriage to Jezebel and how these kingdoms were affected.

Each generation needs kings and queens of the kingdom to fight the good fight and to keep the evil kingdom from taking ground during their time to rule the earth.

The kingly must see their seed or offspring as a high priority to God. We must endeavor to help them discover their gifts and callings. Give them love, support and the experimentation they need to find their purpose and their destiny in Christ. This is a primary role of all kingly. From secretaries to chiropractors, from nurses to brain surgeons, from professors to factory workers, all kings and queens must prioritize our families so the kingdom of God continues to advance. If the church would just keep our own children in the faith then each generation could focus on winning the lost and the church would grow exponentially with each generation.

Our children must know how to have a personal relationship with Christ our King. They must know how to hear and obey His voice. They must know, memorize and be familiar with the kingdom's history and wisdom of God's Word, the Bible. They need to know more than what the church teaches. They must hear us teach biblical principles to them and see us apply the same principles to our lives, so they in turn can apply these values to their own lives.

We, the kingly, are 100 percent responsible to do our best to raise godly heirs. I know they have a free will but we must have a clear conscience before God as to whom we allow our heirs to be trained by, listen to and relate to. Royals are not just anyone; they are special, not of this world, full of destiny. If they know this early on, they can rationalize their training disciplines and understand why they cannot act or behave like heathens.

I think I have made my point. We kings and queens cannot leave all the spiritual training to the priests or the local church. We too are responsible to raise royals. I truly believe that God is a trans-generational successor God. He is the God of Abraham, Isaac and Jacob. He sees down your generational tree. As the kingly, we need to see down that generational tree as well.

We are responsible to see that spiritual character, the ability to learn, relate to others, and be humble is taught by our example, that prayer, fasting and reading of God's Word are normal for royals. This is above providing money for college and cars. We need to teach our children to wear their spiritual garments in their generation. They will encounter battles we will never face. Each generation needs kings and queens of the kingdom to fight the good fight and to keep the evil kingdom from taking ground during their time to rule the earth.

6. Royal Character

Character has been quite the debated issue in the United States through the Clinton years. Because of this, a leader without character our nation suffered tremendously. He confused our children about sex, drugs, loyalty and marriage. Although he may have been brilliant as a politician and speaker, he will be remembered mostly as a president (or king) without character.

Take in drastic contrast the reign of George W. Bush. His character is not questioned. He makes principle-based decisions. Children are not confused by who his wife is and if he loves her. We have not had to protect our kids from news about this president. Character counts not only in our natural nation but also in our spiritual nation.

Our character as Christian men and women is critical. Sadly, kings, queens and priests alike have separated character and Christianity. We live in an emotionally based culture that wants you to feel good rather than be good, to base decisions on feelings rather than character. This has created a real character crisis that has affected many royals. It is from the core of our character that we live, decide, worship and relate. We will demonstrate character to our generations that follow us by our children. It is much easier to grow up from character if you see character modeled.

In an evangelism class I took in seminary, Dr. Fish stated clearly to us young men, "Character is something you are when nobody is around." This means when you are alone, you do not view inappropriate things, have inappropriate conversations, cheat in a business situation or on your taxes. Hebrews 12:1 says heavenly host is watching us. That means our lives are on video before the heavens, so character does count. Having character means your word is good. As it says about the righteous in Psalm 15, he "who keeps his oath even when it hurts" will dwell on God's holy hill. Character is how people are in the church, community, city or their sphere of influence.

Who we are is of greater importance than what we do. If we are faithful and godly over what may seem little, we have advanced the kingdom by a godly life and heritage. We can be responsible for much, but without character, we cannot only lose what we think we have but damage our Lord's kingdom.

I encourage you, if there is an area in your life where you know you are compromising, clean it up willingly. Let our God be glorified and the kingdom advanced through you.

7. A Principled Life of Royalty

Prior to the 1950s, America was a principle-based nation. We made decisions by absolutes of right and wrong, good and evil, righteous and wickedness. In the 1960s, we moved into emotionally based decisions combined with individual relativism. Now we can live as we want to without being judged. Our decisions are assessed by how we feel about them and not what is right and wrong.

Royalty cannot afford such folly. The Christian life of the kingly and queenly is a principled life. Let me explain. This is not religion in any way. It is not a discipline that is put on you externally by someone. Rather a principle-based life is birthed from the inside of you as a response to love.

I love my wife Lisa dearly. I remember when we were in our first apartment that we both worked full-time and I was a full-time seminary student. As a young couple, we had few arguments, but one kept reoccurring almost weekly. The argument was about taking out the garbage.

191

Lisa worked the 8 A.M. to 3 P.M. shift and I worked the 3 P.M. to 11 P.M. shift. One day as I was running out the door, Lisa wanted me to take the garbage out. I was late and said, "I don't know what this garbage issue is about but when I get home we are going to get to the bottom of it."

Well that night we talked about garbage. In my family, we filled the garbage so high that anyone in the family who tripped over it had to take it out. Lisa, on the other hand, specifically remembers her mother walking out in the cold snow of Pennsylvania to put the trash by the curb. As a child, Lisa thought to herself that if her dad loved her mom, he would take out the garbage.

You see Lisa equated taking out the garbage as a symbol of loving her. When I understood this, I willingly disciplined my lifestyle to take out the garbage. She no longer had to yell, question or be upset, because my love for her motivated me.

Discipline is a response to love. As royalty, if we love our God, our spouse, our family, future generations, our cities and our country, we live a principle-based life. Those principles include our conduct toward others, principles of health, wealth and intimacy. We do not *have* to pray; we *get* to pray! We discipline our life to seek God through praying and reading God's Word. For example, we do not struggle with tithing because it is a principle and the right thing to do.

We pray with our spouse and family because we get to. We prioritize quality time with our spouse and family. We vote, we pray for our leaders, we intercede for those in our sphere of influence regularly. We are principled royals.

We know our lives have generational impact. We are not above the principles, rules and laws of our government unless they are directly opposed to our God and His Word. When you are royalty, you accept a principled life willingly.

The Christian life of the kingly and queenly is a principled life.

Imagine if God said, "I want to give you cities and nations to rule in the next world." Wouldn't you live with an intent to train for this? How would royalty think? What would a royal do? People are depending on you. I think prayer would be easy if you had a responsible position.

That is the point of this whole book. If you understand you are royalty and handle the responsibility it carries, it will change your lifestyle from sloppy agape to responsible royalty. Our life will take on a different order when we understand our royal linage. When Christians really know who they are on the earth, it changes them for the rest of their days.

They no longer look just to live for themselves. They live for the city, nation or world that God has called them to. They are, in my opinion, the single most dangerous people on earth. They need no chiding into a godly life. They yearn and cry out for the nature of Christ to be formed in them and for opportunities to give their life away for the cause of Christ in some form of ministry outlet. They are truly moved to meet needs, love, and touch, connect and change the eternal lives of people inside and outside of the church walls.

They are royals and they are armed with the wisdom, power, fear of God, counsel, miracles, prophecy, gentleness, peace, patience and kindness. They are motivated by love so that they can see "Thy kingdom come." Regardless of the cost, they will principle their lives to optimize God pouring Himself into them to advance His kingdom on the earth.

8. Royal Resources

Any American reading this book is wealthy. We are by far the wealthiest nation ever to exist in history. We have grown up with such luxury that even a common person today has experienced luxuries that earthly monarchs 100 years ago never dreamed of. We travel, eat and dress like no other nation in history. I say this to put perspective on our resources.

As royalty, our resources are of the utmost importance. It matters what we do with the finances God gives us, whether we spend money on entertainment or on missions. Therefore, what are our responsibilities regarding wealth? I believe there are three major areas.

Kings in the natural create wealth in some type of fashion. Some learn skills to serve someone as an employee. Others go to school to serve as doctors, lawyers, counselors, massage therapists or mechanics. Still others create business so that they can employ those in need. There are those whose gifts are in art, writing, sports, entertainment or computers. They have the ability to give their time and talents to create wealth.

Some kings and queens create wealth through one income stream, and others develop income through multiple streams, like employees who own rental homes or have weekend businesses or hobbies that generate an income. However, God has gifted you, you are responsible to develop that gift to its fullest.

Your gift is whatever it is. Do not compare yourself

to others or be ashamed of your gift. Issues of faithfulness and character come into play here. God gives, increase it. He may give you ideas to better serve your field or clients. He might inspire you to start a business. He may just be pleased to allow steady growth in a company. However, He blesses you to be creating wealth, be grateful, and responsible.

The second area of responsibility for royal resources is management. Any kingdom whose residents live financially irresponsibly will be weak. You only have to look at the billions we in America have given to prop up irresponsible nations to understand this issue. As royals, managing may be even more important than creating. How the servants of the Bible managed the talent they received determined their master's response and favor.

Our resources are holy. They come from God. He gives us the gifts, He blesses us and provides abundantly. Our responsibility is to manage this abundance so that we can hear, *"Well done my good and faithful servant"* *(Matt. 25:21).*

So live within your means or actually below your means, and do not debt yourself to death. Prioritizing giving, saving ,and investing are very important royal tasks. A myriad of godly resources about each of these topics exists in Christian bookstores. Equip yourself to be responsible with the royal resources you have.

Our third area of responsibility is that of distributing wealth. We are given so we can give. We are blessed to bless others. Remember, *"It is more blessed to give than to receive." (Act 20:35)*

Where to give is just as important because your royal resources have a purpose. What is your mandate from God in your city, state, nation or world? Ask the Lord to tell you where to give. Walk in agreement with your spouse. You can also involve the priestly in your life if you need ideas.

There is so much good to be about in these later days of Christ advancing the kingdom. Find the place and amount and obey the Lord. He is looking for financially obedient royals to move through on the earth to do His will. The distribution of wealth is part of what royals do.

In the federal government, plans enable federal employees to create wealth (taxes, etc.), manage (national budget) and distribute (government programs). As royals, our finances should have a similar structure. I personally find the distribution the most fun. I love when God tells me where to put His money. Then I know I am advancing His kingdom the way a king should.

The fact that you are royalty cannot be changed. You are what you are by a true royal bloodline. What kind of royalty you will be is the inheritance you give your God and your generation. My prayer is that in the areas of knowing who you are, knowing your royal purpose, following royal protocol, accepting responsibility, having a kingly view, royal character and being responsible for your wealth, you will excel and give God your absolute best. After all, the world is depending on you.

XII

The Wounding of Royalty

 o far, all this kingly, queenly stuff has been great. I hope fully you understand what God observes when He sees you. He sees royalty on a mission for the King of Kings. He sees you as gifted, able and hopefully willing to fulfill your ministry as a king or queen on the earth.

Yet there is a place in many of kings and queens that most do not talk about: the wounding they have endured. Sometimes financial, marital, family, church or friends cause great pain. It is the place where not only unpleasant things have happened to good people, but the king's or queen's heart actually gets hurt.

For some it is the public humiliation of bad choices that were made or false accusations that go public. Many of us have heard of a priestly person who has fallen or has been accused and years later had a ministry larger than ever. Kings and queens are no different, although much of the wounding that happens, whether based on truth or not, will afterward produce the greatest years of kingly ministry manifestations. For some, this season of humility or humiliation is just the beginning of a God promotion. For others, it adds a depth or level of passion or compassion for others, or for the ministry.

Unfortunately, the fruit of our wounding may not be clear for a long time, if ever. As a king who has endured several incidents of woundedness, I personally know that it can take a decade before I begin to understand why. I have, however, found that in almost every case, my past wounding has brought life and healing to others in the future.

Let us look at a few biblical examples of woundedness, starting with Abraham. In Genesis 12, right after God called Abram, a famine struck Egypt. So Abram went to Egypt. He told Sarah his wife to lie and say she was his sister. Abram gains financially, sheep, cows, donkeys, camels, servants—he was getting rich on the deal of Sarah being his sister and it probably felt great. People liked him, good things happened and then bam! One of the most powerful people in the world at the time, the king of Egypt, rebukes him for lying to him. Next came the family pain of his nephew Lot becoming a prisoner of war. Then the long aching in his heart for decades due to not having children and not seeing the promise fulfilled. That must have hurt, especially since everyone knew that he had said God would do such a thing. After that followed the pain with Sarah and Haggar and Ishmael. As a father who was promised so many children, to see his first-born leave must have been agonizing.

Then Abraham does the "She is my sister" routine again with King Abimelech. Again, he is questioned publicly before all the officials. Fortunately, even in this mistake God blesses Abraham. Then he had the ultimate test of sacrificing his son Isaac to God. By now, he trusted God, but still this was a long trip up the mountain for King Abraham. The death of his wife also was a heart pain. Kings and queens go through wounding. Some of our own doing, some not of our own, but you can be sure that this is a part of the process.

Another king I want to look at is Joseph. Here is a kingly man who really understood woundedness. He was handsome, smart, and fine and is able to get things done, yet hated by his brothers. He is thrown in a pit, sold to slaves and the newspaper at home reports him dead. To be totally hated and rejected by those close to you in the family and in the family business together hurts. Imagine being thrown in a hole for days and then sold as a slave.

He did nothing wrong, but he was wounded. He rises again to be a leader, with blessing and the favor of his boss Potiphar. Yet hated again by those around him, men who themselves may have been sleeping with Potiphar's wife. Handsome, well-built, now lied about, publicly humiliated and thrown in jail. Talk about a day of wounding. Knowing you have done nothing wrong and someone else perpetuated the crime and you are in prison paying the bill.

However, he guards his heart from bitterness and rises to the top again—even in prison—because of his administrative skills, work ethic and ability to relate with others. Joseph's God-given ability moves him to second in the land. Then the family stuff again with his brothers visiting happens. That resolves well, the family moves to Egypt. Things look good; then Dad dies and the brothers still misunderstand and falsely accuse Joseph of wanting to harm them for what they did to him when he was young. That must have sliced through Joseph's heart.

In this king's life, we can see that wounding is not always our fault. It can just happen and God can still use it to make us more like Him. Joseph did the right things and still ended up in prison. Therefore, if you are lied about, falsely accused, hated for no reason, called impure when your motives were pure, you are in good company, the company of the kingly and queenly.

Next, let us look at a king who God really loved but who also endured wounds. David was another who really was misunderstood by his brothers. David was moving into national awareness by killing Goliath, but his brothers falsely accuse him of being conceited and having a wicked heart (1 Samuel 17:28). That must have hurt, but David's response shows it was not the first time his brothers had done such a thing. "Now what have I done?" David asked. "Can't I even speak?"

Jesus, who led a sinless life, was also wounded along the way.

Things go well for a while and David moves to the palace. He does not do anything wrong, and yet Saul's jealousy leads him to try to harm David. David leaves and lives a vagabond lifestyle being chased for years by a king to whom he has done no wrong. Imagine the pain night after night, sleeping in caves, not knowing what tomorrow brings. Knowing the *Jerusalem Times* is skewing the stories about you because of King Saul. Even when David proves his heart is pure publicly by not killing Saul, Saul continues his pursuit of David.

What pain he must have felt to be attacked by a person he cared for, served, and risked his life for in battle, his father-in-law and a person who God anointed to be king. This attack was family, political, and military and must have wounded the heart of David. Then David moves to the land of the Philistines, a foreign land away from where he was anointed to rule.

His family is stolen; his men want to turn on him (1 Samuel 30:3-6). David and his men rescue their families and shortly after hear of Saul's death. Sometimes the wounding comes moments before God elevates you.

David goes on to be king of Judah, and Israel had a season of victories. Then David wounds himself with lust, adultery, and with his relationship with Bathsheba. David repents, their baby dies and the wounding is incredible. But worse is still to come via David's sons.

Amnon rapes his half-sister Tamar. Absalom vindicates Tamar by killing Amnon. (2 Samuel 13). Then Absalom begins rising up against David and David leaves the palace again. Absalom proceeds to sleep with David's concubines in public (2 Sam. 16). The apparent hurt of Mephibosheth in 2 Samuel 16, a man to whom David showed only kindness, at the time must have seemed like one of the proverbial straws about to break the camel's back. Perhaps the death of David's son Absalom, regardless of his extreme unfaithfulness, did "break" his heart.

The wounding from the counting of Israel's army and the realization that 70,000 people innocently died because of David's sin must have been heart wrenching. I hope you can see the immensity of his woundedness. Again, David at times had no guilt of wrongdoing, but deep pain shot through his heart, for years in some cases. Other wounds were self-imposed or came from consequences of not dealing with family issues. Kings often have incredible wounds of various kinds. It is often part of the territory.

Let us now turn to the King of Kings. Jesus, who led a sinless life, was also wounded along the way. There could have been early family members and friends who questioned the immaculacy of his conception. He grew up in the real world of a business owner. Somewhere between the ages of twelve and thirty his father dies. This hurt the Son of God because Joseph was truly dear and a faithful role model to Jesus in the kingly ministry. Joseph was a self-employed king, who had the ministry of loving Mary, Jesus and the rest of his family while working and attending synagogue.

In addition to the grief of John the Baptist's death, Jesus had to endure the day-in, day-out questioning of His heart and motives from the religious sect. The hurt of being misunderstood was a constant wounding by those doubting Jesus' deity.

Jesus endured the abandonment of the disciple just before the time of His death. Physical, emotional and spiritual mocking occurred prior to His crucifixion. Hanged naked before the crowd on the cross when He had done nothing wrong was painfully humiliating. He was a King who knew wounding like no other.

Isaiah 53:3 describes Jesus as *"despised and rejected by men, a man of sorrows and familiar with suffering."* Hebrews 5:8 reveals that Jesus learned obedience from what He suffered. Sometimes our wounds are a learning experience out of which we can receive something important. Other times it is not just for ourselves to learn, but others as well. Isaiah 53:5 states, *"But He was pierced for our transgressions, He was crushed for our iniquities; the punishment that brought us peace was upon him, and by His wounds we are healed."*

I do not like it much, but I know from personal experience that God has repeatedly used my wounds to heal others. Jesus was wounded for others as well. We can again see how many of the kingly and queenly are wounded during life. It seems to be true that no matter how good we are, pain still happens. Even when wounds are self-imposed or are consequences of bad choices, they are still very real.

You may be wondering what to you do if you are in the midst of a wounding right now. Perhaps something in your family, business or personal life is causing you significant hurt. I want to outline a few guidelines that have been helpful to me.

1. Pray. Ask God if there is anything that is yours to own up to, such as wrong choices, bad attitudes, sin patterns or general lack of love. If He finds something to work on inside of you, let Him do His work. Talk to your pastor in this process. Often involving your priestly minister in a painful time in your life can give you added spiritual insight.

2. Get in the Word. When you are experiencing pain, delve into the Bible more than just once a day. Keep it with you in your car and in your desk at the office. It is so important to have the Word speak to your heart. At times, it will offer correction; other times it will bring encouragement. The Word will wash you and fill you as well as get you through this hurtful time.

3. Worship. This is a perfect time to celebrate God, His goodness and mercy. In the midst of your woundedness, when you least feel like it, lift up your voice and your hands and thank God that He is a good God. Play some worship songs, clear your mind and heart of the issues and focus on Him who is always worthy of praise. It might start slow and with difficulty, but eventually you can make progress until you agree with the angels of how worthy He really is. When I have been wounded (which has been numerous times), worship gets me through the day or night.

4. Submit. I do not necessarily like this step either, but it is very helpful to submit to people who love you and hopefully have your best interest at heart. As long as the advice is godly, try to comply.

5. Record. Get a journal of some kind and write down what you are doing to cope with your situation. Also, use this journal to write down what God is saying to you. Often He talks clearer when we are listening. His words to you can be life.

6. Friends. The need for friends is true at all times but never truer than when you are going through a wounding. As Americans, we live mostly alone, but in the midst of pain, we need to huddle up with friends. Share your hurts, pains and imperfections during this difficult time. This is often when you find out who your friends are. They are the ones who will be there for you when things are not sailing smoothly.

What about all the wounds in your past? I have a couple exercises I think would be helpful.

Cleansing the Temple

The following component is an exercise that I call cleansing the temple and can remove a lot of the pain that you may carry in your soul. This pain may be from your family of origin, such as issues caused by neglect, abuse or abandonment. Some pain carried in your soul is from your spouse. In some Christian marriages, spouses traumatize one another or deprive one another to such a degree that anger appears overwhelming.

The anger builds up in your soul until the size of your wounds appears insurmountable. Even though you did not cause the wounds, you are now responsible to heal from them. Similar to walking outside and being shot by a sniper, you are 100 percent responsible to heal from the wound, even though another may be 100 percent responsible for causing the wound.

This is a very important concept to understand

because in our culture victim status is power. This power is manipulated to make other people pay, or is used to shirk full responsibility for yourself or the direction of your life. I can attest as much as anyone else can to the fact that life can be painful and that some people enjoy creating pain for others. Therefore, I encourage you, if you have wounds that others have afflicted into your life, continue to read and follow the guidelines mentioned.

The "cleansing the temple" exercise has its roots in the biblical examples where Jesus cleanses the temple. The account of this is found in each gospel. You would do well to take a moment and study each account. The recordings in Scripture of this event are as follows.

Jesus entered the temple and drove out all who were buying and selling there. He overturned the tables of the money changers and the benches of those selling doves. (Matt. 21:12)

On reaching Jerusalem, Jesus entered the temple area and began driving out those who were buying and selling there. He overturned the tables of the moneychangers and the benches of those selling doves. (Mark 11:15)

Then he entered the temple area and began driving out those who were selling. (Luke 19:45)

In the temple courts he found men selling cattle, sheep and doves, and others sitting at tables exchanging money. So he made a whip out of cords, and drove all from the temple area, both sheep and cattle; he scattered the coins of the money changers and overturned their tables. To those who sold doves he said, "Get these out of here! How dare you turn my Father's house into a market!" (John 2:1-16)

Every account has within it the principles of the "cleansing the temple" exercise. First, we will review the four major principles, and then walk through the practical application. The following Scripture will be our text for our "cleansing the temple" exercise.

When it was almost time for the Jewish Passover, Jesus went up to Jerusalem. In the temple courts, he found men selling cattle, sheep and doves, and others sitting at tables exchanging money. Therefore, he made a whip out of cords and drove all from the temple area, both sheep and cattle; he scattered the coins of the moneychangers and overturned their tables.

To those who sold doves he said, "Get these out of

here! How dare you turn my Father" house into a market!"
His disciples remembered that it is written: "Zeal for your
house will consume me."

*Then the Jews demanded of him, "What miraculous
sign can you show us to prove your authority to do all
this?" Jesus answered them, "Destroy this temple, and
I will raise it again in three days." The Jews replied, "It
has taken forty-six years to build this temple, and you
are going to raise it in three days?" But the temple he
had spoken of was his body. After he was raised from
the dead, his disciples recalled what he had said. Then
they believed the Scripture and the words that Jesus had
spoken. (John 2:13-22)*

Biblical Principles

Principle 1: The Temple

In the four accounts of Jesus cleansing the temple,
the temple refers to His physical temple in Jerusalem.
However, John's account also refers to Jesus' own body as
a temple. This is the first insight that Jesus was changing the
dwelling place of God from a physical temple to the temple
of a human being. Paul develops this thought a little later

when he records that we as Christian believers are the temple of God:

Don't you know that you yourselves are God's temple and that God's Spirit lives in you? If anyone destroys God's temple, God will destroy him; for God's temple is sacred, and you are that temple. (1 Corin. 3:16-17)

God's plan all along was to dwell inside of us. We are His holy temple. This being true, temples can get defiled through many avenues including manipulations, abuses and neglect from others. When we are defiled through life, our temple gets defiled and needs to be cleaned out as well.

What is interesting here in this passage is that Jesus, the owner of the temple was the one who took full responsibility to clean His own temple. He could have made the moneychangers and sellers of doves who were the perpetrators in the story clean up their own mess, but He did not. He cleansed the temple.

We are the possessors of our temple. If your temple is defiled through the abuse of others, you are the one that needs to clean it up. You are actually the *only* one who can clean your temple.

Even if it was others who have caused the defilement, he or she cannot clean it out of your temple. They can say they are sorry, but that does not get rid of the muck or defilement that has scarred your soul. That mess you need to clean up. I believe Jesus took responsibility to clean His own temple because it gives us a clear message that we can clean our own temple as well.

Principle 2: He Identified the Sin

In the gospel of John, Jesus stated, "Get these out of here! How dare you turn my Father's house into a market!" (John 2:16). The other three Gospels use slightly stronger words: 'it is written,' he said to them, '"My house will be called a house of prayer," but you have made it a den of robbers.'"

Jesus was letting them know what the offense was, the reason why He was cleansing the temple. They were taking something holy and misusing it to profit for themselves. Most of the people who have hurt you have no concept of your holiness or preciousness. You have felt used or abused during the incidents where you were wounded. In one of the exercises of cleansing the temple, we will need to identify the sin or damage that has been done unto you by those who have defiled your temple.

Principle 3: He Engaged His Anger

Jesus was able to engage His anger at the injustice both physically and verbally. His turning over the tables was probably quite a scene. I am sure that is why the Jews asked Him about His authority to create such a ruckus.

This was not just Jesus having a bad day. This was an act of His will. Jesus thought through His options and acted in obedience. This is an important point to understand because it will be an act of your will to clean your temple. Once you walk through the rest of the exercises, I believe that it will be an act of obedience as well.

Some have asked me how I know this was something Jesus premeditated. Look at John's account of the cleansing of the temple. *"He found men selling cattle, sheep and doves, and others sitting at tables exchanging money. So He made a whip out of cords"* *(John 2:14-15).* In this verse, you get the feeling that Jesus is looking around and witnessing the people's mistreatment of His holy temple. Then in verse 15, he gets a bunch of cords and takes the time to make a whip. Now I do not know how long it took Jesus to make a whip, maybe minutes or hours, but it shows me that He had intention on using that whip and committed some premeditated time before He went in to cleanse His temple.

As we go further on in this exercise, you will also be making choices to prioritize your time to prepare for cleansing your temple. Those who do go about this intently have received great breakthroughs in their life.

Principle 4: Temple Restored to Original Order

Jesus' cleansing of the temple offers a picture of how to heal your wounds inside your own temple. After he engaged the righteous rage, His temple was cleansed. Remember only He could cleanse His temple. No other prophet or king has done so before Him or after Him. He alone could clean His house, as only we alone can clean our own temple.

Practical Application

I have seen many wounded souls over the past fifteen years while working with couples and individuals in both inpatient psychiatric hospitals and outpatient office settings. These wounds are at the core of their being. Many of these kings, queens or priests have experienced trauma in one form or another.

The person that has experienced a trauma has experienced it in all three levels of their being: spirit, soul and body. All three parts have been defiled, injured or neglected.

If the trauma affects all three dimensions of a person, doesn't it make sense that the healing must involve all three aspects as well?

While training therapists across this country I explain these three levels. Then I ask them, "Why do we just treat trauma cognitively and expect people to heal? If the trauma affects all three dimensions of a person, doesn't it make sense that the healing must involve all three aspects as well?" Of course, the answer is yes.

I tell you this because some of you will presume to have forgiven someone, only to discover the bullet is still inside your heart, so your wound still festers. Muck and defilement are still surrounding this wound. That does not mean you did not forgive them necessarily, it just means you have not cleansed your temple yet.

The concept I am about to suggest to you may seem foreign or uncomfortable at first. My experience with cleansing the temple is nothing short of miraculous. I have seen sexual abuse survivors heal very quickly after this exercise. I have seen women who have been sexually betrayed by their Christian husbands suddenly be able to move through the stages of grief and forgiveness so much quicker than those who refuse to cleanse their temple. I have seen people hurt in business or by lawyers able to recover.

What I would encourage you to do is keep an open mind and try this exercise if you feel others have injured you. After (not before) you do this exercise, you can tell if it has been effective or not.

1. Write an Anger Letter.

The first step in the cleansing of your temple is to choose someone on your list of people who has hurt you and write an anger letter to him or her (never send it). I often tell my clients to imagine this person in the room and unable to talk or move. You can say whatever you need to him or her in this letter. This is **not** a letter to suppress but rather let out all the thoughts and feelings of hate, disgust and anguish that has been robbing your soul. This letter is not an "I forgive you" letter. That is later. This is the place where you get to rid yourself of the anger that has been a part of your soul. Someone wounded acts a lot differently in life than someone who is healed. I know from experience. This first step is to simply express your anger in letter form toward the person who caused you pain.

2. Warm Up.

In Jesus' situation He made a whip for himself. I do not recommend whips, but a padded baseball bat or racket could be helpful. Firstly, warm up your body. Take your bat and hit your mattress or pillow first with small hits then medium, large and extra large hits. I recommend you do this three consecutive times. Then warm up your voice as well. Using the word "no" along with the hits, do small, medium, large and extra large "no's" with your voice while hitting. This may feel awkward but removing this buildup of pain out of your soul and spirit feels almost like having a baby so you want to be physically warmed up.

While you are warming up, you may want to make sure you are home alone and I would also disconnect the phone so that you are not disturbed.

Note: Before doing this, if you have a heart or other medical condition that warrants talking to your medical doctor first, please do so.

3. Read the Letter Out Loud.

After your physical warm up, take the letter you wrote to this person and read it aloud. If the person's name were "Toby", then you would read the letter a loud such as this: Toby, how could you have done this to me? I trusted you! ...

Now of course Toby is nowhere around. You certainly do not need to do this with him or her around. You are simply in a room alone just reading the letter aloud.

4. Engage the Anger Physically and Verbally.

After reading your letter you can put your letter down and pick up your bat. You can hit the bed or pillow and let "Toby" symbolically have it. You can yell, scream, cry but let the wounding out that has been robbing you. You can symbolically tell him, "Your secrets are not controlling me anymore and you are to blame for my pain!" You have no limits as to what you can say to this person. For once, let go of all the control that is keeping this wound infected. Let it out!

This can last anywhere from fifteen minutes to an hour. Usually your body will let you know when you are done spiritually, emotionally and physically putting this behind you.

You are worth getting it all out. Someone has given

you something toxic. You have been unhealthy ever since. After you remove this poison from your system, you will feel so much better. Trust me: Kings and queens who have done this have felt so much better. This really works if you actually do the exercise.

Comments

When you do your "cleansing the temple" exercise, you should only work on one person at a time. If three different people have offended you, then you must complete three different cleansing the temple sessions. **DO NOT** do just one exercise to address all of the people who have offended you. Each "bullet" needs to be taken out separately.

What I tell clients is to start with the least painful trauma and work your way up to the larger offenses. This way, you get better skilled at the exercise and will know what to expect.

Each person you work on may give you different experiences or even insight. I've know some men and women who thought person number three was going to be the worst, and yet someone who had caused a smaller offense actually proved more difficult to work on. As kings and queens, take a moment, make a list and then schedule time to cleanse your temple. A clean temple is easier for God to work through on the earth. I have done this several times to stay clean.

Forgiveness

This stage of healing is only for those who have already completed the hard work of cleansing the temple. If it has been five days or longer after confronting your anger, you are probably feeling better already.

In my experience it is similar to being able to breathe normally again after having a cold. I can feel the junk in my lungs is gone and can breathe clearer and easier now. I have had several clients tell me after doing the "cleansing of the temple" exercise regarding their mom or dad, the next time they spent time with their parents they were not all knotted up or tight inside.

The next step to healing is forgiveness. I am not suggesting that you look up your violators and tell them you forgive them. Rather I am talking about doing another therapeutic exercise so that you can see how far along on the forgiveness issue you really are with this person.

The following exercise is very effective and most are able to choose to forgive the people who wounded them. The Scripture is full of teachings regarding forgiveness. You can get a concordance and look up all of the verses, beginning with Matthew 6:14: *"For if you forgive men when they sin against you, your heavenly Father will also forgive you. But if you do not forgive men their sins, your Father will not forgive your sins."* Continue working your way through the rest of the New Testament regarding forgiveness. I realize for some individuals that healing and cleansing has to come first in order to move toward forgiveness from their heart. For a book on the subject of forgiveness I would recommend *The Bate of Satan* by John Bevere. This book goes into great detail about the importance and value of forgiveness.

This exercise guides you through the process. Therefore, you can forgive and have a place in time where you know it was released from your soul. You can walk through this with all of those who are on your list. This might include your dad and mom, spouse or others who have hurt you. This exercise has three steps to it. So pick one person and go through this process. Again, I recommend you do this exercise while you are home alone. You will need two chairs.

Forgiveness Exercise—Step One

Face the two chairs toward each other. Pick a

chair and sit facing the other chair. We will call the chair you are sitting in Chair A.

While you are sitting in Chair A, role-play as the person who hurt you. As you role-play this person, have him or her apologize and ask for forgiveness for all that they have done to you. They are hypothetically confessing to you in the other chair (Chair B). If I were doing this exercise about my dad I would sit in Chair A. I would role-play my dad, and I would verbally own the (his) sin and apologize and ask for forgiveness for the things I did and did not do to Doug in Chair B.

As I play my dad I might say, "Doug, I need you to forgive me of...." Now since I am playing my dad, I can say what he needs to say in order to own and apologize for the sin in his life toward me.

Forgiveness Exercise—Step Two

Now I just played my dad as he asked forgiveness of several things while pretending Doug was in Chair B. I heard symbolically my dad own his sin and ask for the forgiveness of it. Now I can start Step Two, where I physically get up and sit in Chair B as myself.

After hearing my dad ask for forgiveness, I now decide how I will respond. Above all be honest. If you are not ready to forgive, tell him. You could say, "I'm just not ready to do this yet, but I will try again in a few weeks." Whatever you do when you play yourself, do not be fake or just say what you think you should; instead be real.

If you are able to forgive your offender then tell him so. As in our example, Doug is now talking to Dad in the opposite chair. I could say, "Dad I forgive you." In addition, I could really let him go for his abuses or neglects of my soul and their affects on my life.

If you are able to forgive, move to Step Three. If you are not at this time able to forgive, get your calendar out and set up a time when you will try this exercise again in about three to four weeks. Repeat this monthly to measure your progress.

Forgiveness—Step Three

In our example Doug has forgiven Dad. Now I physically get up, sit down in the Chair A again, and play the role of my dad. Doug has just forgiven him. Now it is Dad's turn to respond to Doug's forgiveness of him. Dad (role-played by Doug) might say, "Thanks Doug." When Dad is done talking to Doug, the exercise is over. So in brief:

⊙   Step One—Start in Chair A as the person who hurt

you asking for forgiveness.

⊙ Step Two—Now sit in Chair B as yourself and honestly respond to this person's request for forgiveness.

⊙ Step Three—If you have forgiven him or her go back to Chair A and play the person who hurt you responding to the forgiveness.

Forgiveness—Comments

This can be a very emotional exercise for those with extremely abusive backgrounds, so have a box of tissues nearby. Also make sure the phone, doorbell, etc. will not interrupt you. It will be important for you to stay focused.

Remember to do this exercise only after you have completed the "cleansing of the temple" exercise. So many Christians try to forgive before they cleanse their temple. Jesus cleansed the temple before He issued the words, "Father, forgive them" found in every Gospel account. Cleansing comes first, then forgiveness.

Remember in all these exercises that each person gets their own time in the chair with you. Each person who hurt you needs to be role-played as apologizing to you. Again, I do not recommend that you role-play more than two people in a day.

Releasing the people who hurt you *will* free you up if you complete your "cleansing of the temple" work first. I have personally experienced much freedom in these exercises that God showed me. I did not read about these exercises somewhere and Christianize them. I believe that these are exercises the Lord gave me in the process of healing myself so that I can help others heal also.

You are kings and queens and the more healed you are, the more life of God you can participate in. The world needs you healed, they need life-giving kings and queens. Wherever, whoever has wounded you, I encourage you to heal.

I pray in the name of Jesus for all who are reading this and need to apply these exercises to their life, that You bless them as they feel and process their woundedness. Comfort them, Lord, and guide them to still waters so they can drink of the intimacy that You have for them. In Jesus' name, Amen.

XIII

Trust Me

he issue of trust is so critical in any relationship. As a Christian counselor I can attest that this is definitely true. In a marriage where trust has been injured it takes time and consistent behavior from one or both parties involved. This is especially true if they both want the marriage to work.

As in any marriage, the husband has his perspective of what the issues are and who needs to change and often how they should change. The wife has her perspective and experience as well as to what is wrong, who should change and how. In my counseling office I spend little time on blaming games. This type of behavior leads to more damage than growth in the relationship. As a Christian counselor and author, I specialize in restoring relationships. More often than not the love and personalities are not the main issue. The structure or lack of structure is often the culprit of unhappy marriages.

Let us face it, kings and queens and the priesthood are in a relationship together similar to a marriage. We are joined together for this mission to have spiritual children, raise them and hopefully they in turn will reproduce spiritual children as well. As ridiculous as it would be for someone to try without scientific help to impregnate himself or herself, so also would it be to think kings or queens or priests by themselves could birth or raise children of God. We are created to fulfill different roles and when each does their part, the kingdom advances. When they do not, growth is limited and strife abounds.

Let us face it, kings and queens and the priesthood are in a relationship together similar to a marriage.

So what kind of gripes does this God ordained couple have to deal with? The kings feel controlled often by the priest. They feel the priest decides the family government and it is usually a monarchy of priests. The priests decide if they (the kings) are good, smart, holy or loyal enough to do even the simplest of ministries like ushering in a local church.

They complain that the priestly decide their family's goals, missions and methods of how this family is run. The kings complain feeling financially used. They feel that they give the resources but no input or gratitude is there for all the hours of hard work these sacrifices represent.

The priests in turn complain that kings think because they give their tithes that they can control everything. They feel that their work in the ministry is discounted and not thought of as "real work." They complain that the kings do not follow through financially when they make verbal or written pledges to support the church or ministry. This dashes the hopes and dreams of the priest and makes them feel that kings are untruthful.

We are created to fulfill different roles and when each does their part, the kingdom advances. When they do not, growth is limited and strife abounds.

You can see how much fun this couple might be in a counseling session, each thinking the other should change. In reality both often need adjustments to optimize the ministry of our King Jesus in a local church or national para-church ministry.

So how do we get through this? As individuals, if a king, queen or priest, has hurt you, it is your responsibility to seek healing for yourself. I recommend you follow the anger and forgiveness exercises in the wounding chapter. Both the kings and priests need to heal. If both persons in the relationship release their hurt, anger and unforgiveness, healing is possible and then the two can rebuild trust. It will be difficult to heal the kingly and priestly relationship if there is pain in the soul of your being.

As kings and queens, take the first step toward reconciliation. Do not wait for the other person to change first. Lead the way and be an example of the ministry of reconciliation that Christ has given to you. Humble yourself to your priest at the present time or any other past priest that you have sinned against. Honestly and humbly, go to the pastors you have had over the years. Check your heart and your behaviors. Check to see if you had ungodly attitudes, beliefs or behaviors toward them or their ministry. This is when you do your heart's inventory not theirs. Even if you believe that they have sinned against you greater, keep your side of the street clean so to speak. If you deal with your side of the offense at least you will have a clear conscious so that trust once again has the best chance to spring up.

As kings and queens, take the first step toward reconciliation.

I have seen many, many miracles over my years as a counselor when couples choose to humble themselves and ask forgiveness. It may feel awkward but it works! If there are any priests who are reading along, the same process works for you if you have had attitudes regarding parishioners, laity that are less than what they represented themselves as, or if you have discouraged kings and queens as they desired to do ministry. If it is an individual offense, go to the individual in your present or past church. If it is a corporate attitude of not empowering kings and queens, repent publicly!

I will never forget the church I was in when teaching an Intimacy conference. They held me over to preach on the following Sunday and as I delivered a sermon about getting out of the boat, I went heavy on the king's message. The pastor and I had already talked about this. He was excited because his church was starting a cell group system similar to New Life Church in the next week or so.

When I asked how many in the congregation were willing to walk into their kingly calling, over 70 percent of the congregation came forward to the altar. I asked the pastor to pray over his hungry for ministry flock. Before he prayed he asked the congregation for forgiveness of any behaviors or attitudes of his that made them feel they were lesser people than church staff ministers were. They forgave him, he prayed and it was just like a great marriage counseling session! There was so much rebirthed love and trust for each other.

We got rid of the anger, unforgiveness and sin, so what is next? Well, the rebuilding and developing agreements on how things are going to be run in our local church and para-church ministry. Who makes what decisions? Are we in a priestly or kingly monarchy where one person or a small group makes the rules? I have heard horror stories and success stories with all forms of government. Are we a corporation where certain areas are totally the priestly decisions and other areas are 100 percent the kingly decisions? This corporation style can or cannot work depending on the individuals involved. How about a true democracy where all vote or you can vote in those who will decide. This can work but you have to decide who is hearing from God or you will have a system with differences of opinions on how God can work.

Now kings and queens also must decide how the priestly will play a role in their life, business and decisions.

Do you consult your priest, do you honor their spiritual discernment in you life and business? Do you verbally, in writing or with gifts thank your pastor or priestly when their lives and words made thoughts clear for you? We need each other and the quicker we understand this the better. Neither is superior, we are equal yet different. When we accept and appreciate the differences we can have an abundance of spiritual children and duplicate quickly while awaiting our Kings return.

Now that we have cleaned up the past and made agreements on how we are going to treat and respond to each other, we can move forward. This can only mean much happiness, accomplishment and connection within the body of Christ. I think we will truly attract more and more kings, queens, and priests to join us in the kingdom.

Now that we love each other till death do us part and we have all these spiritual babies, what about the future? How will we prepare for them and their future generations?

I want to lay out a dream. A dream that has not been practically worked out yet but discussions are brewing. I want to share a dream for the happily married kingly and priestly body of Christ in this and the next generation.

I imagine a church much like the legendary King Arthur dreamed of Camelot, where nobles lay down their swords, their titles, their wealth and their pride. They agree to honor and protect each other. They are friends in word and deed. This is a church that can rise up in kingly strength and priestly compassion, and change continents with the practical and aggressive love of God. The nations are ready for the united body to take their rightful place on the earth.

You say that is a dream, I agree. Today it is a dream but I believe my God is a dream fulfiller. He fulfilled Abraham's dream for a family, Joseph's dream of leadership, David's dream to be a king and numerous prophets' dreams over and over again. He even fulfilled the Son of God's dream to have an eternal bride. I believe He can fulfill this dream on a local and national level.

So how can this be practically accomplished? Right now I am only hoping that kings, queens and priests can and will fully trust each other. When a couple marries, one of the expressions of trust or lack of trust shows up in who handles the money and how the financial decisions are made. The couple may agree on financial democracy, but whatever they agree on they will have a financial government established by vote or tyranny.

What if in a local city like where you and I live this vision could come true? What if beyond the tithe and local church giving that a city-wide trust was established? In my city it could be the Colorado Springs City Trust Fund.

The money of this fund would go to local ministries advancing the kingdom through evangelism or meeting the practical needs of people as well as giving to national and international ministries and missions. What if this city trust, which is a legal entity, consists of members of the priestly along with the kings/queens of all levels who regularly give of themselves as well as their church? The members elect a board of the trust annually that is equally kingly and priestly. For the disbursement of funds, there would have to be a majority vote for whatever they decide to do with the trust. The kings and queens would love a trust where they are represented and their ministry passions are considered. The priests can be empowered to release and bless ministries that are outside the walls of their church and honestly feel a part of something bigger than their own church that is also reaching their city for Christ.

When you get kings, queens and priests together, nothing is impossible. When you bring the authority that kings are given by God in their city and the influence that pastors are given you have combined resources not bound by a church agenda and you now could start anything. Feed it long enough to fund itself if possible, and target specific needs in your city, nation and world.

One church might not be strong enough to do a

certain ministry but a city trust with kings and priests together could do anything. The ministry opportunities are endless. When kings and queens are really given the task to take their city for Christ, they charge like bulls.

When you get kings, queens and priests together, nothing is impossible.

I think this dream is doable. I can only imagine if small towns had such funds. The kings and queens would tell other kings and queens, the priests would tell other priests and more could be done in a year together than a decade of divided kingly and priestly ministry.

Dare to dream! We do not desire a Camelot; we desire a kingdom not of this world to take over the hearts of those who live in our cities. It is our commission to see it done. So as kings and queens, let us honor and trust our priests. They in turn can trust us and together we will birth more spiritual children, which will bless both the kings and the priests as they hear Jesus say, "Well done my good and faithful servants."

12My command is this: Love each other as I have loved you. 13Greater love has no one than this, that he lay down his life for his friends. 14You are my friends if you *do what I command. ¹⁵I no longer call you servants, because a servant does not know his master's business. Instead, I have called you friends, for everything that I learned from my Father I have made known to you. ¹⁶You did not choose me, but I chose you and appointed you to go and bear fruit—fruit that will last. Then the Father will give you whatever you ask in my name. ¹⁷This is my command: Love each other. (John 15:12-17)*

XIV

Jesus as King

 e read in Scripture that Jesus is King of kings. It is easy for us to see Jesus as king, especially since he is God. We know He is ruler of all before coming into time and space with us and He will always be King throughout all generations. He is always King.

I want to talk about Jesus as a kingly minister. His life is one to be studied as you enter into your kingly or queenly ministry. Let us start with his lineage. Jesus was from the kingly tribe, Judah. Remember the blessing of Jacob to his son Judah in Genesis 49:10:

The scepter will not depart from Judah, nor the ruler's staff from between his feet, until he comes to whom it belongs and the obedience of the nations is His.

Jesus' tribe was kingly in as much He was not from the Levitical tribe to be a priest, but rather from a kingly tribe to be a kingly minister. In Matthew look at the linage of Jesus from Abraham (King) to David (King) to Joseph a king. Seeing Jesus as a kingly minister is important for us to see ourselves in the light of Jesus. Many of us come from kingly heritage, as did our Savior. He is so much like us in many ways.

Let us look at Jesus' kingly family of origin. Joseph, Jesus stepfather was definitely a king. From a practical standpoint, Joseph was a self-employed business owner. He had customers, stock to keep, payables to keep up with; and employees were most likely his sons including Jesus.

Joseph was a man who obeyed God. Remember when Mary was pregnant. This was disgracing to him. He knew they had not been intimate together. He had no reference to believe in an immaculate conception. The angel told him in a dream to take Mary as his wife and he did it. In Matthew 2:13-14 we read a second account of the angel telling Joseph to leave and take his family and business and move to Egypt. In Matthew 2:19 an angel tells Joseph to move back with his family to Israel. In verse 22 he is warned in another dream and goes to Nazareth. Each time God spoke to Joseph it records his immediate obedience. He did not consult a committee or ask anybody. He just obeyed God. Remember part of Jesus' training was watching his stepfather Joseph obey God without hesitation. This is a great thing for our children to see.

I remember when I was living in Fort Worth, Texas, I went to Colorado Springs for a white-water rafting trip and to do counselor training. That weekend God spoke to me in the World Prayer Center saying that He wanted me to move my family and counseling practice to Colorado Springs. I went home shared this with my wife and eight weeks later we were there. I had to explain to my children Hadassah, then six and Jubal, four years old that God told me to move our family and business. They were right there when we looked for our house, office and their school. Children learn from what their parents do.

Jesus could have easily watched Joseph obey God as they moved from Israel to Egypt, back to Israel, and to Nazareth. Joseph just did what God said even if it did not make sense in the natural (marrying a pregnant woman, relocating his business). He was an obedient man of God and as a kingly minister he definitely was a great role model for Jesus to see obeying even if it seems radical.

Joseph worked hard. You do not relocate a business twice (from Israel to Egypt, Egypt back to Israel) and not work hard. You have to get new customers, find supply chains, distribute your product and build a reputation each time. Everyone who has their own business knows the start up side is the hardest. Jesus was right there in the middle of all these changes and saw God supply the needs for Joseph, Mary and the family. Jesus sees growing up with Joseph a righteous man, a patient man (remember Joseph was not intimate with Mary until after Jesus was born), a man led by the Spirit and obedient to God's commands. Jesus also saw day in and day out a hard working and probably smart businessperson.

Let us look at Jesus' training as a first-born son in a family business. Although I am sure Mary and Joseph spent many hours teaching Jesus the Scripture, praying together, going to the synagogue, and attending the various holy day ceremonies, there was more to Jesus' training than religious aspects. As the oldest son he has to learn Joseph's business. If you have ever been around a family business, you tend to start "employment" early. It is not hard to believe even as a boy getting pointers on carpentry by Joseph. As a teen it is easy to believe in that culture much of Jesus' training for His kingly ministry was on-the-job training.

Day in and day out Jesus training for the kingly ministry was mostly perspiration, not inspiration.

Remember Jesus worked in an era before power tools. Day in and day out Jesus training for the kingly ministry was mostly perspiration, not inspiration. He was not off in a private school learning philosophy. He was shaving wood, carving trees, planning wood and nailing things all day long. Remember where he was living was not exactly the coolest places in the world either, in Egypt and Israel. These were hot places where hard work, lots of sweat, drinking water, and living more like a construction worker than scholar took place. Kingly training is often hard work.

As I speak to kings and queens who have significant influence your training was most likely also similar to Jesus'. They worked hard, long hours for many years. Their training was the marketplace. They had to buy equipment, deal with banks, have ups and downs, good customers and bad, good breaks and bad ones, legal issues, taxes and all the things God uses to make kings and queens out of you.

There came a day when Jesus' training for the kingly ministry went up a notch. Somewhere between twelve and thirty, Joseph the great kingly example was dead. After feeling the pain and loss, it was now Jesus' turn to run the family business. This was a significant part in Jesus' training. He went from being a great hardworking employee of the company to the owner.

Jesus spent by far the largest portion of His life in the carpentry business, preparing for His miracle ministry of three years

Jesus now has the full weight of making sure the company did well enough to feed his mother and brothers and possibly their wives and children. Jesus had to be the dealmaker. When a guy wanted five tables in two weeks, he had to encourage the whole group to agree to the long hours of hard work. He had to do the books or at least know the money situation. He had to negotiate prices on wood, tools, storage space, office location and expansion. He was now the man who had to make difficult choices when it came to employees and the quality of work. This does not even bring into play the family issues with his brothers. How would you like to grow up with a brother who never sins? How much fun could that be, or even worse, to work with a person who doesn't sin? Take it a step further: How would you like to work for your brother, who is your boss, who never sins! I am sure there were lively conversations, especially because of the things the family knew about Jesus' birth and how special He was. I say this to illustrate that part of Jesus' kingly training had to do with relationships.

He had to have great relationship skills to run a profitable business, keep business coming in and manage customers and employees. He was being prepared as much in His relationship training as He was in the day in day out hard work and sweat of the carpentry business.

Other things you learn in a business you own is the value of delegation, employee training (discipleship) and watching others come into a place of higher skill. You learn how to encourage in order to see greater potential. All of these were trainings in Jesus' kingly ministry. Jesus was not off in a seminary learning about God. He was day in day out having to apply spiritual truths to customers, business employees, and yes, to how to make a profit.

Jesus spent many waking hours teaching how to make a table, door, steps or whatever was needed and how to make enough money to pay for the mortgage of property or rent money, food, clothes and saving for future business purchases. Most people do not think Jesus ever touched money. Jesus understood how to make profit, He had to be trained about money enough to keep the people he loved fed and working. You feel a lot of responsibility financially when you are the owner of a family business.

Let us look again at this training for the kingly ministry of Jesus. He trained in the marketplace as we discussed by sweat, hard work and persistence for probably fifteen to eighteen years. If He started at age twelve, this would mean God trained Jesus for eighteen years in this manner. Jesus spent by far the largest portion of His life in the carpentry business, preparing for His miracle ministry of three years.

I say this so that some of you, who are sweating at work, dealing with employees or bosses, have responsibilities of owning or working for a company, you are being just like Jesus. That is just the process of kingly ministry. God does not send you to philosophy school but rather the marketplace to develop your kingly ministry.

It is here where your character is developed. You may be tempted to take short cuts, you develop a work ethic, learn negotiation and compromise, how to organize your time and energy, how to make money, to be patient with coworkers, learn to love people not like yourself, be falsely accused, not liked, misunderstood, in need of miracles, understand spiritual warfare, fast and pray, intercede and behold the many deliverances and practical miracles. Our God promises to build up your faith so that you have a personal relationship with God to tell others about Him.

You do not have to give up the training ground of the marketplace to go into a Levitical or priestly ministry. Although some are truly called to this Levitical ministry most of us are not. Most of us are the net to catch and minister to the people in the marketplace. You have a high ministry as kings and queens. Imagine when the person at work is sick and has no hope and you, just a regular supernatural king/queen minister prays for them, and they get well instantly. They know it was not you, it was God.

What about as you go through your days with loving behavior in the midst of marketplace rudeness? Others see you as different. What about the marriage you pray for that stays together? What about the team member in your kid's soccer team whose parents are saved one day when you share the gospel with them during a Sunday soccer game?

The miracle ministry is ours. We are closest to the need. As we have faith that we are chosen for these miracles and that we are righteous because we are righteous in Christ's blood we will also realize that God listens to our royal prayers.

We do not have to go to a healing crusade to see miracles. Just practice and when the time comes God will give you clarity of your kingly ministry in the world. For sure we know that the greatest kingly ministry of all is to love others. Jesus was the greatest example of this. This is a miracle, the ministry to love.

You cannot love without being with God the Father in prayer, filling yourself with His words. Anyone, no matter how long they are saved, can love people. Any king or queen can love and that would be a great ministry in this world today.

As we looked at Jesus and his training for the kingly ministry, let us look at Jesus' friends, the disciples, to see how they were trained for their own kingly ministry. Remember the Christian priestly cast did not occur until later in church history. Let us look at the disciple's kingly training for their ministry.

Peter is familiar to us all, but let us look at his training. He had a fishing business. This merchant business was important in this day. He was a food merchant. He spent his time on the water, caught free fish and sold them to make a profit. Talk about hard working and smelly days, long nights, and early mornings. Peter had stock in which he had to sell each day. Fish do not keep long in Israel's heat without refrigeration. Peter then had to sell all these fish to a mostly Hebrew consumer. Peter hustled for a living. He worked hard sometimes with success, sometimes with no results. He was dependant on God and the sea to feed his family, make boat payments, and see that his children had their needs met. Remember the first miracle Jesus did for Peter was to throw his nets down after a long unsuccessful night. They caught so much fish they needed help. This was a marketplace miracle that meant a financial windfall for Peter and company.

¹One day as Jesus was standing by the Lake of Genesee, with the people crowding around him and listening to the word of God, ²he saw at the water's edge two boats, left there by the fishermen, who were washing their nets. ³He got into one of the boats, the one belonging to Simon, and asked him to put out a little from shore. Then he sat down and taught the people from the boat. ⁴When he had finished speaking, he said to Simon, "Put out into deep water, and let down the nets for a catch."

⁵ Simon answered, "Master, we've worked hard all night and haven't caught anything. But because you say so, I will let down the nets."

⁶When they had done so, they caught such a large

number of fish that their nets began to break. ⁷So they signaled their partners in the other boat to come and help them, and they came and filled both boats so full that they began to sink.

⁸When Simon Peter saw this, he fell at Jesus' knees and said, "Go away from me, Lord; I am a sinful man!" ⁹For he and all his companions were astonished at the catch of fish they had taken, ¹⁰and so were James and John, the sons of Zebedee, Simon's partners.

¹¹Then Jesus said to Simon, "Don't be afraid; from now on you will catch men." So they pulled their boats up on shore, left everything and followed him. (Luke 5:1-11)

This business training savvy and dependency on God was part of Peter's training as one of the lead disciples of Jesus. It seems Jesus liked those who were trained by the fishers; trade. In Matthew 5 in this same incident as in Luke 5, Matthew states Jesus called Andrew, Peter's brother, as well as James and John, who were also fisherman. Hard workers make for great kingly ministers.

Then there was Levi, a tax collector who was working for the government and making money off other people. Now here is a person who understands negotiation, people and how to make money. Again, Levi was a king, not a priest by vocation.

14As he walked along, he saw Levi son of Alphaeus sitting at the tax collector's booth. "Follow me," Jesus told him, and Levi got up and followed him. 15While Jesus was having dinner at Levi's house, many tax collectors and "sinners" were eating with him and his disciples, for there were many who followed him. (Mark 2:14-15)

And so on goes the list of disciples that all were kingly ministers trained by the marketplace, taught by Jesus, filled by the Spirit and changing human history.

The kingly is who Jesus was on the earth for as well as the priestly. Jesus in choosing His team brought a group of kingly types together and taught them the kingdom so they could experience it themselves. Remember He sent these kings out to heal the sick and cast out demons. He knew if they could be confident in how things worked in His kingdom that they would duplicate it in Jerusalem and throughout the world.

Jesus is definitely a great example of the kingly ministry, which includes His kingly lineage from the tribe of Judah, his kingly family with Joseph and Mary, his training in the family business as employee and employer, his kingly team and his kingly commission to go to the ends of the earth.

Jesus is kingly as many reading these pages are also kingly and queenly. God has a holy, royal calling on your life to be about His ministry to seek, love and minister to those in all areas of our spheres of influence. God is the one who trains us for His ministry through us. Trust me; He is calling for you to royally touch your world with His love and service. He desires to touch others with your life. Remember pew sitting is not a Christian ministry. Pew sitting is just enough to rest and inspire you to greater outreach in your life. As you practice your kingly ministry, the ministry of worship, declaring the Word and worship through giving life becomes much more meaningful to you.

I hope you are encouraged to reach your royal destination in Christ. The thing you need to know is that you are royal and that you have a kingly or queenly destination within your sphere of influence. Therefore, with the same fervor Jesus received His training and releasing into His kingly ministry, I encourage you to seek your God-given kingly or queenly ministry.

More Materials by Douglas Weiss, Ph.D.

Intimacy: A 100 Day Guide to Lasting Relationships: Dr. Weiss walks couples through the skills necessary for lifelong, intimate relationships. This guide can transform couples to deeper levels of intimacy. **$21.95**

Sex, Men and God: Every Man's Road map to Successful Sexuality: Ninety-five percent of Christian men today have not received sexual guidance from their father. This book offers men the knowledge to be sexually free, a better lover to their wife and passes down a legacy to their sons. **$13.99**

The Final Freedom: Pioneering Sexual Addiction Recovery: Many Christian men are silently struggling alone with sexual addiction. This book brings practical insight for men to help themselves or their friends find lifelong freedom from sexual addiction. **$22.95**

Passion for Purity: This video has almost 90 minutes on spiritual, soul and body, male sexuality. Many men have testified to being sexually healthier and free just by watching this video. **$29.95**

Sexual Intercession: Winning the Battle Over Lust: This video connects the dots between our sexuality and our spiritual authority. This video clearly gives the why behind staying sexually pure. **$19.95**

Best Sex for Men/Women: This video gives men/ women a straight forward sex talk. Each person learns how to be a godly lover and resolve years of sexual frustration that builds up in many marriages. **$29.95 each**

Good Enough to Wait: This is the sex talk you would get if your dad was a sexuality researcher and Bible teacher. Dr. Doug gives your teen practical insights to motivate them to stay sexually pure until their wedding night. **$39.95**

Shepherding Your Sons Sexually: Every man wants to know what to say to his son about sexuality. This video gives guidelines that men can apply and give his son a great chance of becoming sexually successful. **$29.95**

TO ORDER CALL 719-278-3708!

Heart to Heart Counseling Center

Douglas Weiss,Ph.D., Executive Director
5080 Mark Dabling Blvd.
Colorado Springs, CO 80907
719-278-3708

Free Newsletter

Kings and Queens are welcome to join our free newsletter
via e-mail. Weekly you receive a short scripture lesson
from a kingly and queenly perspective. As you grow in
your royalty, and as a Christian this newsletter can
strengthen you. To register go to:
www.ministryofkings.com

Counseling

As the Executive Director of Heart to Heart Counseling
Center, Douglas Weiss, Ph.D. and other licensed counselors offer telephone counseling to anyone needing help in
their Christian walk. To set up an appointment with a
Christian counselor call **719-278-3708**.

Conferences

Dr. Doug Weiss travels nationally and internationally providing conferences to strengthen the body of Christ. These
conferences include The Ministry of Kings and Queens,
Marriage Conferences, Men's conferences and others for
your local church. To schedule a conference call **719-278-
3708**.

Contributing Authors

Ted Haggard is the senior pastor of New Life Church, an 11,000 member congregation in Colorado Springs, Colorado. He is also the President of the National Association of Evangelicals and the author of seven books including Primary Purpose and The Life Giving Church.

Dennis Doyle is the CEO of the Welsh Company. He and his wife Megan are also conference speakers on the subject of marketplace ministry. Dennis is the founder of Hope for the City in Minneapolis, Minnesota.